Senior Management
and Quality

Also available from ASQ Quality Press:

We Move Our Own Cheese!: A Business Fable About Championing Change
Victor E. Sower and Frank K. Fair

Making Change in Complex Organizations
George K. Strodtbeck III

*Lean Acres: A Tale of Strategic Innovation and Improvement in a
Farm-iliar Setting*
Jim Bowie

*Making Change Work: Practical Tools for Overcoming Human Resistance
to Change*
Brien Palmer

*Office Kaizen: Transforming Office Operations into a Strategic
Competitive Advantage*
William Lareau

The Quality Toolbox, Second Edition
Nancy R. Tague

Root Cause Analysis: Simplified Tools and Techniques, Second Edition
Bjørn Andersen and Tom Fagerhaug

The Certified Six Sigma Green Belt Handbook, Second Edition
Roderick A. Munro, Govindarajan Ramu, and Daniel J. Zrymiak

*The Certified Manager of Quality/Organizational Excellence Handbook,
Fourth Edition*
Russell T. Westcott, editor

The Certified Six Sigma Black Belt Handbook, Third Edition
T.M. Kubiak and Donald W. Benbow

The ASQ Auditing Handbook, Fourth Edition
J.P. Russell, editor

*The ASQ Quality Improvement Pocket Guide: Basic History, Concepts, Tools,
and Relationships*
Grace L. Duffy, editor

To request a complimentary catalog of ASQ Quality Press publications, call
800-248-1946, or visit our Web site at http://www.asq.org/quality-press.

Senior Management and Quality

How to Leverage Quality for Profit

Fin Rooney

ASQ Quality Press
Milwaukee, Wisconsin

American Society for Quality, Quality Press, Milwaukee, WI 53203
© 2018 by ASQ.
All rights reserved. Published 2017.
Printed in the United States of America.

23   22   21   20   19   18   5   4   3   2   1

Library of Congress Cataloging-in-Publication Data

Names: Rooney, Fin, author.
Title: Senior management and quality: how to leverage quality for profit /
    Fin Rooney, MBA, B.Sc. (Eng.), C. Eng., ASQ CQM/OE, CQP MCQI, MCMI.
Description: Milwaukee, WI: American Society for Quality, [2018] |
    Includes bibliographical references and index.
Identifiers: LCCN 2017052438 | ISBN 9780873899659 (hardcover: alk. paper)
Subjects: LCSH: Senior leadership teams. | Quality assurance.
Classification: LCC HD66.7 .R66 2018 | DDC 658.4/013—dc23
LC record available at https://lccn.loc.gov/2017052438

Director, Quality Press and Programs: Ray Zielke
Managing Editor: Paul Daniel O'Mara
Sr. Creative Services Specialist: Randy L. Benson

ASQ Mission: The American Society for Quality advances individual,
organizational, and community excellence worldwide through learning,
quality improvement, and knowledge exchange.

Attention Bookstores, Wholesalers, Schools, and Corporations: ASQ Quality
Press books, video, audio, and software are available at quantity discounts with
bulk purchases for business, educational, or instructional use. For information,
please contact ASQ Quality Press at 800-248-1946, or write to ASQ Quality Press,
P.O. Box 3005, Milwaukee, WI 53201-3005.

To place orders or to request ASQ membership information, call 800-248-1946.
Visit our Web site at www.asq.org/quality-press.

♾ Printed on acid-free paper

Quality Press
600 N. Plankinton Ave.
Milwaukee, WI 53203-2914
E-mail: authors@asq.org
ASQ   **The Global Voice of Quality®**

* * *

Contents

List of Figures and Tables

* * *

∗ ∗ ∗

Preface

The whole area of quality is one that has undergone significant change in the last 50 years. Many new ideas and philosophies have been promoted, and many have fallen out of favor. Others have been superseded or improved.

Quality can be a nebulous concept at the best of times, but in the business world, it has also had a very restrictive meaning—usually one related to product quality. Because of this limited definition, the area of quality has usually remained under the function of Operations, and thus has not been sufficiently leveraged for the competitive advantage it can generate.

The aim of this book is:

- To give a strategic overview of quality for senior management;
- To show how the core concepts of quality can help improve organizations;
- To give senior managers the data not only to hold beneficial reviews among their colleagues, but also to hold useful discussions and reviews with those further down the organization chain;
- To revisit our thinking on quality—what it is, what its function is, who is responsible for it, and how it should be measured.

Some of the questions covered in this book include:

- What is quality?
- How can we use quality and the Quality department to improve our organization?
- How can the Quality department interact with other departments to generate improvements?

- Should there be a separate Quality department, when most of us would agree that "quality" should exist in all departments? Does the mere existence of a Quality department create a silo culture, where all non-conformances tend to be seen as the responsibility of the Quality department?

- What is the role of a Quality department if everyone is responsible for quality?

- How can we best use the Quality department in our dealings with suppliers and customers?

This is not a book about quality tools and techniques, though some of these are briefly discussed. There is a whole industry publishing these on a monthly basis (just like management and leadership publications). This does not mean that some of the new ideas are inferior; my concern is that the new tools are often added to existing ones, and I feel there is scope to *replace* some of the existing tools with better ones.

The book has a bias towards manufacturing, but I have tried to cover the service industry also. It is my hope that readers can apply the ideas, information, and examples to their own organizations, whether manufacturing- or service-based.

Also, although this book focuses on quality, some of the main themes can be applied to other support functions such as Human Resources, Health and Safety, Environment, and IT.

I have used the abbreviation QA (Quality Assurance) to refer to the Quality department.

NOTES

1. As a strong supporter of continual improvement, I am open to suggestions and comments from readers who wish to let me know about errors or omissions from this book. I would also be grateful if readers were to send me their own thoughts on what is expressed in this book, their own lessons learned, or examples from their own experiences. I will credit any information used.

2. Much of this book is written from the viewpoint of what senior managers need to know about the next level down; the intention is that by exploring this level, senior management will:

   a. Have a better grasp of the issues and opportunities at that level;

   b. Ask the right questions of their subordinates; and

   c. Be able to use this book and the answers from subordinates to focus on issues and continually improve the organization.

APOLOGY

I have worked in quality for more than 30 years, in manufacturing and service industries, and attended many quality training sessions and seminars during that time. I have read many articles, blogs, books, and comments and interacted with some excellent quality professionals. Unfortunately, in many instances, I did not note the source of a particular article, comment, tool, or definition.

I apologize in advance for not crediting these appropriately. If a reader makes me aware of the correct source, I will include it in future printings.

✳ ✳ ✳

Introduction

Do you find yourself feeling more and more annoyed with the quality and continual improvement industry? It seems obsessed with creating tools, techniques, and acronyms such as TQM, SPC, QFD, Six Sigma, 8D, FMEA, PPAP, Pareto analysis, MSA, APQP, 5S, TOC, JIT, and BSC. When I read articles on quality, I often see individual authors creating and describing new tools, usually prefaced by: "this is something I call 'TLA' (Three Letter Acronym)." Is there any other area where so many tools and techniques are used, and new ones seem to appear regularly? Maybe the quality industry has an inferiority complex, and thinks that by coming up with new tools, it will keep itself relevant. But quality is simple.

> *The goal of quality is simple—find the best current way*
> *of doing something and keep doing it, while looking for better ways.*
> *If something goes wrong, fix it so that it doesn't happen again*

The quality industry seems constantly to re-invent the wheel, tweak it in some way, and then give it a different name just to confuse us. Improving the tools used is of course a positive thing, but sometimes having too many choices can be as bad as too few, increasing the chances of not picking the most appropriate tool or technique.

This book is not about giving you a list of tools and guiding you through the use of each one. Rather, this book takes a higher-level look at quality, investigating some of the misconceptions that surround quality, teasing out how an organization can benefit from quality initiatives, and simplifying the implementation of a strategy with quality as a core element.

In addition to the numerous acronyms, the quality industry also seems to be obsessed with using Japanese terms for many quality-related concepts (*muda*, *gemba*, *jidoka*, *poka-yoke*, *kaizen*, etc.). Why is this? Can you think of any other business function that would do this? Would a finance or purchasing department come up with such terms? Is it not clearer for most English-speaking people to have the words in English? The cynic in me wonders whether some people in the quality industry are trying to create a jargon-based and elitist approach to quality, which is further supported by the whole Six Sigma "belt" framework. For me, one of the key functions of a Quality department is to simplify, not confuse with acronyms, foreign language terms, and jargon. But there always seems to be a new bandwagon to jump on, and there is no shortage of articles written about quality and introducing even more acronyms.

I hope that in this book you will find a leaner approach to quality, one that:

- Has minimal jargon;
- Contains practical steps you can implement;
- Will result in a rethink of how Quality is evaluated; and
- Delivers benefits to you as a senior manager and to your organization.

Let's start with a little quiz:

When you think of your Quality department, how many of the boxes would you tick in Figure 1?

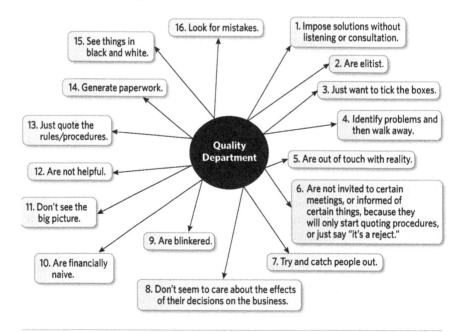

Figure 1 Quality department diagram.

Maybe you ticked all of the above? I'm sure there are many other items that could be added to this list, but at the same time, I would hope that things have improved since the "bad old days."

In fairness, there are many occasions when the Quality department (QA) is viewed as having a positive influence and effect, but I still think many of the above comments are ingrained in people, including senior managers. Maybe you can your ask your colleagues for their opinion of this diagram. Do many of them tick several boxes? If they do, what does that indicate?

The most annoying thing for me about the diagram is that:

- Several of the statements are probably correct, and

- Quality personnel are themselves to blame for people having these opinions.

One of the main aims of this book will be to address these issues so that by implementing the ideas proposed, you won't want to tick any of the above items—or at least not as many.

CHAPTER ONE

* * *

What Is Quality?

CHAPTER OUTLINE:
In this chapter, I look at the word *quality*. I discuss high-level definitions of quality and some of the related concepts. I look at what is a "quality problem" and at what quality is not.

Defining quality would seem to be a hard task. A person who looked online, read books about quality, looked at online discussions and forums, read quality journals, or attended quality courses or conferences would find a multitude of definitions, and most of them are valid in their own way. Why is this? Why does it seem much easier to define other terms such as "health and safety," "environment," "finance," "marketing," "production," and IT? The reason, in my view, is simple—*people are trying to define something that does not exist on its own.*

> Quality, *as a word, should not exist on its own.*

The word *quality* must be associated with other words—quality of product, quality of process, quality of service, quality of design, quality of marketing, quality of transaction, quality of response, etc. Splitting the word *quality* out on its own has caused it to become indefinable and has simultaneously created problems that have been with us ever since. It may have been done with the best of intentions at the time, but it created many problems.

For many organizations, quality is about more than just product or service (see Figure 2).

Is this a good quality restaurant? For a restaurant, as with most organizations, it is the overall package that matters; being bad in one aspect contributes to a bad reputation overall. A diner might come away with a bad opinion if the staff are unpleasant, if the toilets are dirty, if the music is too loud, or if the lights are so low that you need a flashlight to read the menu. There are many ways for a restaurant to acquire a reputation for bad quality—it doesn't just depend on the food.

This is the broad thinking needed when looking at our own organizations; we should not be looking at our products or services alone. We must look at *all* customer interactions—with Sales, Marketing, Quality, Customer Support, Technical Support, Online Sales and Support, After-sales Personnel, Account Managers, Delivery Drivers, and so on. Each time any one of these interacts with a customer, there is potential to devalue the company's reputation. On the upside, these interactions can create an opportunity to enhance our reputation. Knowing this, why do we not spend more time training everyone who deals directly with customers? It's because we are stuck in a certain way of thinking—that our reputation is all down to product or service quality alone. Some organizations try to limit contact with customers, saying that only Sales or Marketing or Quality can contact the customer, but the reality is that other departments (e.g., Finance and Shipping) are in contact with customers every day, so that approach is not going to work.

We have all been customers in poor restaurants or hotels. Do you suppose the owners ever ask someone to go in anonymously and rate all aspects of the business? How many organizations actually act on feedback and comment cards? I have lost count of the number of times I have filled in a hotel comment card, but only once have I received a reply. Does the card reach the appropriate person, or is it "filtered"? If it's filtered, that's another problem that must be addressed.

Figure 2 Restaurant quality example.

The next question is, have we asked someone to review *our* business? Do we follow up on comment cards or suggestion boxes, if we use them? Are we afraid of what someone might find? Are we afraid of criticism? Have we just assumed we are OK? Whatever the answer, where are the data to back this up? I'm not saying it's necessary to have a comment card or suggestion box scheme, but if we do have one, we should have made that decision consciously.

With the advent of online reviews and feedback, we can find ourselves in a situation where people can post a bad review for anyone to read. Do we have a policy of how to deal with this, especially if the review is false? Even if it's true, how do we want to address it—directly with the individual, through a forum, through a review response?

If a person works in finance or sales or customer service, do we not want them to do "quality" work? In fact, do we even define what represents good quality work for all functions or roles? It should be defined, especially if we believe "quality is everyone's responsibility" and "we want a quality culture." These slogans mean nothing on their own; nothing improves because of a slogan. Improvement requires education and training, it requires alignment of people's goals with strategic goals, and it requires leadership from the top. It must be translated into something measurable and, most importantly, it must be implemented. One way this can be done is to include "quality" as part of everyone's annual objectives (and other areas such as Health and Safety objectives, IT security, and environmental considerations).

Many organizations do all of this, but miss one vital point—they measure improvement from the organization's viewpoint, rather than from that of their customers. This will be discussed later on, when I talk about objectives in more detail. Obviously, organizational objectives are needed, but we should not forget to look at things from the customer's point of view. This applies to all departments, not just those that directly communicate with the customer. Every department has customers—internal or external. Internal customers may be the next to receive the document, information, or product, but they are still customers, and processes should be structured with this idea in mind:

- How can each process be set up so that only good product or service gets to the next step?

- As a double check, how is the next step set up to detect whether something has been done incorrectly at the previous step?

From an internal point of view, these two steps, properly implemented, cover the basics of how to provide good products or services. If something does go wrong, they provide a built-in double check to detect the problem before it goes to the external customer. This is what I mean by keeping things simple. Organizations don't need Six Sigma black belts, or statistics, or graphs to figure this out. What is needed is applied common sense and a desire to strip out unnecessary work and form-filling.

Starting with the basic premise that everyone wants to do a good job (or at least that nobody wants to deliberately do a bad job), then our job as managers is to provide the system (including training, infrastructure, tools, and knowledge), to ensure this happens. Those who don't agree with this basic premise will probably end up spending most of their time monitoring and micromanaging people rather than managing, leading, and generating improvements. (See McGregor's Theory X and Theory Y for a good illustration of these two approaches.)

Even when people are doing their best and doing what they think is right, communication can be skewed. In the example of the restaurant with good food but slow service, a front-of-house manager might be inclined to say, "The kitchen is not run properly; we need a new chef or kitchen manager." The owner might say, "I won't accept slow service— either it improves or someone will lose his job." And then the owner might add, "You are the managers; take care of it."

So far, so good, you might think. But if the restaurant owner and managers are serious about tackling the problem, they should be meeting regularly and discussing these issues. When they meet to discuss the poor service, the chef might say, "The service is slow because I need four ovens and I only have two." Further probing might identify that the kitchen manager's hands are tied because the owner has put a freeze on all capital equipment spending for the rest of the year. After discussion, it will be obvious that if customers are dissatisfied, one solution would be to allow additional capital spending. The manager was just following orders; he was told there was no money for capital spending, and there ends the matter. Communication is the key.

And what would happen if the restaurant were big enough to have a Quality (QA) department? The issue would come to the department eventually, they would investigate and ask questions, they would draw up their report and give it to the restaurant manager. Then the restaurant manager might say, "but the owner says there is no money for capital spending." The report does not get to the owner.

Part of the problem is that often issues are not put in terms that matter to senior managers—financial terms. If one of your managers says to you, the restaurant owner, that, "we have about 10 people leaving our restaurant," you might think, "that's not good." But if that same manager says, "we're losing about $300 a night because of poor service," you might be more inclined to take notice, especially if that person then says, "we need three more ovens. The cost of these is $60,000 but the payback period is only 200 days." At that point you can frame the extent of the problem and the solution, and make a business decision.

> *Management is about enabling people to do a good job.*

Related to the "what is quality" question is another question. Is there such a thing as a "quality" problem? Most of us would say "of course there is," and then proceed to pass customer complaints, supplier problems, and internal rejects to the QA department. In reality, the question requires further analysis. This is where ownership is lost, because the problem moves from being a quality problem to effectively becoming a Quality *department* problem.

We need to narrow it down. We should be asking a more detailed question. Is there such a thing as a logistics problem, an invoicing problem, a service problem, or a purchasing problem? I think most of us would answer "yes" to this. But something happens when a customer complains, or when something fails on a production line; the issue goes to the QA department and inefficiencies and lack of ownership begin.

But if problems are directed to the relevant department, instead of automatically to the Quality department, it becomes easier to manage; by looking at the responsibilities, roles, and key performance indicators (KPIs) of the relevant department, the issue can be assessed against these.

Before going any further, I want to clarify two points:

1. I am not saying the Quality department has no responsibility or should not be involved when things go wrong.

2. I am not saying the department that reports an issue is responsible or is the root cause of the problem; the responsible department can only be determined after investigation.

So we need to stop calling everything a quality problem. We must be much more specific. By being specific, we will be clearer as to who should be the owner of the issue and who else should be involved. This will improve communication and speed up resolution of the problem. QA department personnel may well be involved, but unless it's an issue they caused, they should not *automatically* be the drivers of actions required to prevent recurrence. If they are the only drivers, the organization will be stuck in the past, where Quality department staff are seen as the quality police, the bringers of bad news, the sole problem solvers, and the last people to inform when something goes wrong. The QA department's role should be to offer suggestions about ways to address issues and about tools and techniques to improve performance and prevent recurrence, and then to help the responsible department investigate the issue and implement corrective action.

So What is *Quality*?

For the purposes of this publication, I will restrict the definitions of *quality* to those few shown below. Many more definitions appear in Appendix 1, just for reference. These many definitions exist because the word *quality* has been made to stand on its own. In this list, it is clear that because the definitions have no context, any of them could apply or not apply, depending on the circumstances.

Of all the definitions and descriptions that abound for the word *quality*, four encapsulate the main concepts (Figure 3).

What is noticeable is that the first two definitions are more strategic, more generic, and more readily transferable to any area or department of an organization, while the latter two are weighted toward product or service quality. They *can* readily be applied to support or back office functions.

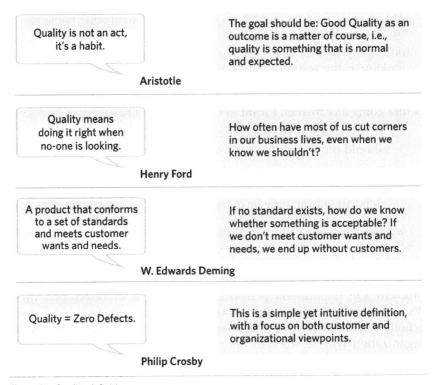

Quality is not an act, it's a habit.

Aristotle

The goal should be: Good Quality as an outcome is a matter of course, i.e., quality is something that is normal and expected.

Quality means doing it right when no-one is looking.

Henry Ford

How often have most of us cut corners in our business lives, even when we know we shouldn't?

A product that conforms to a set of standards and meets customer wants and needs.

W. Edwards Deming

If no standard exists, how do we know whether something is acceptable? If we don't meet customer wants and needs, we end up without customers.

Quality = Zero Defects.

Philip Crosby

This is a simple yet intuitive definition, with a focus on both customer and organizational viewpoints.

Figure 3   Quality definitions.

Another Definition of Quality

My own definition of quality, in terms of manufacturing or service, is that *quality is fundamentally an attitude*—the attitude to do the job right.

It hardly needs saying that people must be properly trained, must have the right tools and environment for the job, and must *want to do the job right*, but it is up to management to provide the right training, tools, and environment.

> *Quality, in manufacturing or service, is about attitude.*

If we agree with this definition, then it stands to reason that the recruitment process should be geared toward detecting this attitude. Skills can be learned, but attitude is not so easy to instil or change in someone if it is not there at the start. If people have the right attitude, then everything else (continual improvement, efficiency, and effectiveness) cascades from this. It is better to have someone with less experience but the right attitude.

Has your organization defined what quality means? Does/would such a definition apply to the product or service only, or could it be applied to all departments? Do individual departments define quality for their activities? It is only by doing so that we can begin to embed quality across the organization.

It's not just our organization's attitude that is important. Customer and supplier attitudes are equally relevant. If our customer doesn't care much about quality, then our own quality level often drops because we know we can let questionable product out the door. It becomes very hard to claw back from that position (we may need to when we start working with a new customer) because the first thing people will say is, "well, the customer accepts it like that and the customer is always right." This cliché has been around for many years, but in fact the customer is *not* always right for several reasons:

- Customers (especially consumers) often do not have the technical capability or equipment to determine whether we have used the correct components or the correct quality of components that make up a product.

- Customers (especially consumers) don't usually conduct an audit of our product or service delivery to see whether we are using cheap labor or paying below the minimum wage.

- Customers may not know what they want until it is in front of them. How often do we go to a shop and see something new that we want to try or buy, or respond to an email or TV advertisement?

- Customers might be purely driven by price, and can end up buying substandard or dangerous products as a result.

- Customers can have unrealistic expectations of how long something will last or under what conditions something can perform.

The bottom line is that where we have a quality standard, we should stick to it, even if the customer doesn't ask for that standard. This forms part of our organizational culture (and will protect us to some extent, if a customer makes a claim). A quality standard gives us some protection from business risk.

If our *suppliers* don't have the right attitude, our choices will be to continually monitor their products or service (which means extra cost for us), spend time working with them to bring about sufficient improvement, or find a new supplier.

When we look at the second part of Deming's definition above (about meeting customer wants or needs), it is clear that these can be harder to define, and we often find ourselves starting to use words such as *features*, *benefits*, and *value*, which themselves can be hard to explain.

Quality and Product Features

Customers often buy a product or service based on price *and* features. Features might include things like reliability, specifications, color, shape, material, or ease of use, but features often get incorporated into the concept of product or service quality, which can be a mistake. A self-parking capability in a car is a great feature, but it tells us nothing about the quality of that car.

Features are usually considered at the design stage of a product or service, and are often beyond the scope of Operations or the service provider to alter.

Features can also be described as those characteristics of a product that encourage a potential customer to buy, and from this we can see that features should be a major consideration for the marketing department. We just need to be careful that we don't add so many features that the product or service becomes excessively complicated, too expensive, or more liable to failure. Extra features can cause a lot of problems from a manufacturing point of view: the product can be difficult to assemble and test, it can mean purchasing component parts that sit in stock for a long time, and not all features might be compatible simultaneously. Adding extra features can also impact after-sales service costs or spare parts stocking costs.

Do you conduct a periodic review of your product or service features or options, to see whether they are all still required by customers, or are there some that are never used? This might allow you to save money by eliminating some of the points mentioned above.

Quality and Benefits

Benefit is what a customer gains by using a product or service. The gain could result because something is cheaper, more fully addresses their needs, or offers customization. The benefits offered by a product or service are ultimately determined by the customer or end user. Sales will tend be better if the focus is more on benefits than features, since the reason customers want a product or service is because they have a need or desire for something that is not being satisfactorily provided. Being close to the customer is crucial for our long-term success because we have a better chance of identifying those required benefits.

Has your organization ever done a comparison between the features and benefits determined by employees or managers within the organization, and then compared those results with the features and benefits reported by customers? This can yield good insights into what's important to customers—the key features and benefits—and help you identify areas of mismatch between the organization and the customer.

Quality and Value

Value is another one of those hard-to-define words. It has different interpretations depending on whether you are the buyer or seller.

Value, like quality itself, must be defined within a context (a particular product or service, a particular customer, a particular market). The classic illustration of this is cars. Is a cheap, reliable car better value than a more expensive reliable car? They both get you from point A to point B, they both protect you from the rain.

Value is ultimately in the eye of the customer, not the organization, so a mechanism is needed to identify what customers value in relation to what we sell.

When we look later at lean management, terms such as *value-adding* (VA) and *non-value-adding* (NVA) are used. For me, these are misnomers; an operator fitting a wheel to a car would usually be classed as a value-adding activity, but customers don't pay for the fitting of the wheel, they pay for the final car (with the wheel fitted). Value, from the customer's viewpoint, does not consist in how the unit is assembled or how the service is developed; this is purely the manufacturer's or service provider's concern, and instead of calling it value-adding, it should be classified as an activity for which the customer can be charged. Complying with regulations or getting certified to ISO 9001 are not value-adding activities, but they can be unavoidable costs when operating in certain industries, or they may be needed in order to bid for business. These are activities that can either be treated as an overhead cost or absorbed into the product or service costs.

Value has several definitions. Here are a few:

- Value = Benefits / Cost
  - Variation 1: Value = Benefits – Cost
  - Variation 2: Value = Quality / Cost

There are several variations of this basic definition:

- Value = Benefits – Cost – Hassle to buy
- Value = Benefits – Effort – Price – Risk
- Value = Benefits – Effort – Price – Risk + / – Treatment

There is a problem with these formulas. Although they look nice and simple, they rely on factors that are themselves hard to quantify. How do we assign numerical value to benefits, quality, hassle, risk, effort, and treatment?

To further complicate matters, value is perceived differently by different customers and different regions, and even by the same customers at different times. If we receive a report that quantifies value, it should be treated as a guide or as a comparison, not as an absolute monetary amount.

Quality is more than our product or service

It is important to remember that quality is not only about the product and services provided by us to the customer or end user, it is about everything that is done within our organization and everything that is done in relation to any external organization. Every manufacturing organization has a service aspect, including transporting goods, invoicing, HR, IT, marketing, supplier visits, and audits.

Service errors in a manufacturing organization can take many forms. An accounting department invoices incorrectly so an organization doesn't get paid on time. A marketing promotion offers various features on a product, but later determines that they are not all possible on the same item. A human resources department recruits someone who doesn't actually have the qualifications listed on the resumé. Or there can be issues relating to transport, packaging, manuals, technical support, customer service, installation, service calls, and so on. Quality should be defined for all of these areas and departments. If it's not defined, measured, and monitored, then how do we demonstrate each department is performing in a "quality" way?

A Few Words About What Quality is Not

As the quality performance of many organizations improves, the low-hanging fruit of product, process, or service improvement diminishes. This low-hanging fruit consists of improvements that are quick or cheap or easy to implement and that generate large savings; it later becomes more expensive for an organization to eliminate the last few errors—the items that are more expensive to fix and generate smaller savings.

Quality is not perfection in all aspects, at any cost. No organization has an infinite amount of money to throw at a problem. We must use our resources wisely. For a business, the goal is the best quality products and services at a profit.

Quality is not "posters on the wall." I think the best thing that can be done with these posters is to discard the text and keep the photos. If all it takes to motivate people is to put posters on a wall with a few slogans, then many psychologists, professors, lecturers, and management thinkers could have retired years ago. (For the flip side of this, there are some very funny *de*-motivational posters at www.despair.com).

Quality is also not limited to World Quality day/week/month. That almost gives the impression that quality is ignored the rest of the time. If you have to have a special time to emphasise quality, then you're losing. Do we ever hear of world finance day or world purchasing day? No, because it's not necessary. I appreciate that in many organizations, the Quality department or senior management use these events to put the focus back on quality and promote the importance of quality, but in my view, quality should permeate everyone's daily job and should be built in to everyone's processes and job specification, so special events are not necessary.

Put simply, anything that wastes resources (including time and information) is poor quality, and this is where there is a clear link between quality and lean philosophies.

> *Any process that wastes resources is poor quality.*

There has been a movement in recent years to look at quality management in terms of risk management. After all, poor quality presents a risk to an organization. The risk might be litigation, fines, or more mundane costs such as scrap, rework, or missed ship dates. Risk management is covered by ISO 31000 (Risk management—principles and guidelines), is included in ISO 9001:2015, and is briefly addressed in a later chapter.

Ultimately, we need to change our understanding of Quality so that we realize that *Quality is not a department or role.* It has to become *how things are done around here.* Creating a "Quality department" has led most organizations to believe that Quality departments are responsible for quality. This fallacy is dealt with in more detail in later chapters.

CHAPTER SUMMARY

In this chapter, we looked at the word *quality* and explored why it should not exist on its own in a business context. We discussed what a quality problem is, and how the vagueness of that concept causes confusion and a tendency for issues to become the responsibility of the Quality department. We then talked about some definitions of quality. There was a brief discussion of quality and how it relates to features, benefits, and value, then we looked at what quality is not, before finishing on a generic view that anything that wastes resources is not quality, and that quality is not a department or role.

Questions

1. How would your senior management team define quality for their areas of responsibility?

2. Has a comparison ever been done between the features and benefits defined by your organization and those of your customers? What are the critical features and benefits, as defined by your customers?

3. Do you perform a periodic review of the features or options offered, to see whether they are all being requested by customers? Or are there some that are never used, potentially allowing you to save money?

4. Does everyone in your organization know that quality is important to the senior management team? How is this actively demonstrated? How often?

CHAPTER TWO

* * *

Quality and Strategy

CHAPTER OUTLINE:

In this chapter, we look at the link between Quality and business strategy, and at how an embedded Quality approach can help you develop and implement an agreed strategy.

Strategy is an overarching approach to planning for an organization. Quality should be viewed in exactly the same way, and for every plan, project, or product, we want to ensure it is conceived and executed in a "quality" manner. When we consider strategy, we want to:

- Look at each plan and each option in terms of:
  - Assessing the internal and external environment—the market, the competitors, the trends (be careful of hidden assumptions).
  - Assessing the internal and external risks to the organization (be careful of hidden assumptions).
  - Assessing the current state of the organization—the strategic analysis; conducting a SWOT analysis.
  - Conducting gap analysis—current versus future state.
  - The outputs of the plan—the decisions and actions that arise from formulating the plan (the strategic plan itself); matching the organization's capabilities to the external environment.
  - The customers of the plan—which stakeholders are affected, how should the plan be communicated, when should it be communicated—and determining whether customer buy-in is essential before executing the plan. Effective implementation often requires ownership. Ownership in turn often requires participation in the process.

- Consider the social, technological, economic, and political (STEP) aspects and impacts.

- Ensure the plans are safe, ethical, environmentally friendly, sustainable, practical, commercially viable, and not least, profitable. Not all of these will apply in each case or for each organization.

Our strategic plan should link with or become our "distinctive competences," those things that we feel give us competitive advantage. Embedded quality is a key part of that. If we develop an attitude of continual improvement in our organization, we will have an organization that will adapt to changing environments, will be utilizing our employees better (with associated improved job satisfaction), and will produce better results, no matter what department or type of organization is concerned. But we first need to break free of the thought process that equates Quality with product Quality. Quality is so much more than this.

Strategy is often about managing change, is generally outwardly focused, and usually has uncertainty in it. This sounds quite similar to various aspects of quality. These areas of similarity are shown in Table 1.

As another example of how Quality interacts with strategic thinking, let us look at one of the most famous models, Porter's model of competitive forces (Figure 4). We can see how Quality applies to these forces.

A. The market

There is rivalry in the marketplace among existing competitors. Quality is very often a differentiator or a perceived differentiator. It features heavily in advertising and promotion. Better quality applies to the service as well as the product.

B. Threat of new entrants

New entrants to the market can bring cheaper products or services, higher quality products or services, or combined products or services. To protect ourselves, we can get ourselves registered to various standards, we can get patents and copyrights, we can try to influence the development of standards, and we can emphasize where our quality exceeds that of the competition and why that is important. We can also aim for a low cost, high quality product or service, one that will make it harder for a new entrant to match or beat.

Table 1 Strategy and quality.

Area of Interest	Considered as Part of Strategy	Considered as Part of Quality	Tools or Techniques Used in Quality
Internal environment	Y	Y	Internal audits; weekly, monthly reviews of KPIs.
External environment	Y	Y	Supplier assessments, customer feedback and complaints, developments in quality, regulations and standards.
Risk management	Y	Y	Failure Modes and Effects Analysis.
Change management	Y	Y	With quality, the goalposts are always changing, so change management is a key component of a good quality program. Can use tools such as Force Field Analysis.
Gap analysis	Y	Y	Measuring performance against targets; setting new targets.
Stakeholders	Y	Y	Liaison with suppliers, customers, and all internal depts.
STEP considerations	Y		Looking at new technological developments, more economical ways of doing things.
Safety	Y	Y	Doing things 'in a quality way' includes doing things safely.
Ethics	Y	Y	Doing things 'in a quality way' includes doing things ethically.
Environmental considerations	Y	Y	Processes that operate efficiently and effectively are more likely to use fewer resources than those that are not.
Sustainability	Y	Y	Sustainable processes give more long term confidence to the organization.
Practicality	Y	Y	Quality has to be practical; otherwise it is just a theoretical exercise.
Commercial viability	Y	Y	Quality cannot ignore commercial realities—it cannot be quality at any price.

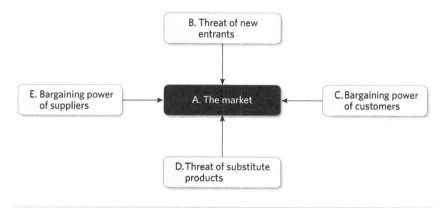

Figure 4   Porter's model of competitive forces.

C. Bargaining power of customers

Customers will often try to negotiate a lower price, and this is where a high quality product or service can serve us well, because it can justify why our deliverable merits a higher price. This is even more effective if we can show the decreased lifetime costs (e.g., maintenance and service costs) of our products and services compared with competitors, and how organizations are actually saving money in the medium to long term. In the business-to-business environment, we can also emphasize the enhancement to our customers' reputation by using high quality, reliable, and long-lasting products and services.

D. Threat of substitute products

Substitute products or services can be difficult to foresee. Often new industries develop that do not seem to have any crossover to our industry, only to have a big impact later on or when used in conjunction with other products or services. Quality can help in innovation, both in ensuring that the development time is kept tight, and that resulting new or modified deliverables are better in terms of product or service quality, delivery, manufacturing time and methods, or reliability.

E. Bargaining power of suppliers

Where suppliers have a lot of power, it helps if we can reduce our dependence on them through better use of existing materials, logistics, utilities, or processes. Quality can help improve the efficiency of the use of these. Where we decide to look for alternative sources, the QA department can help in the selection and assessment of new suppliers. The Quality department should also be involved when considering "make or buy" decisions.

The above are examples of how using QA to its fullest can help our strategy in the market. Senior management should be explaining to all departments, including Quality, the organization's strategy for the coming years, and then explicitly asking each manager to suggest ways they can contribute to that strategy. Often, only a few departments are actively involved (Finance, HR, Operations, Supply Chain Management, Sales and Marketing, R&D), and this is an opportunity missed. Departments such as Quality, Production/Manufacturing Engineering, Maintenance, and IT can contribute positively toward the achievement of an organization's strategy, and senior management are ignoring good resources if these departments are not involved. Inter-departmental teams can identify new sources of revenue generation or cost savings that might not otherwise be realized.

This will benefit the organization in terms of cost savings, improved margins, reputational enhancement, reduced risk, and improved stability—all those things that senior managers strive for anyway. Much of what I'm saying is already happening, but what I propose is that formalizing the quality approach, using material from this book, can improve current strategic thinking and decisions. "Quality" merits a place at board level because it can help create and deliver value to the business, and we should not confine Quality to only our product or other deliverable. Quality directors and managers are usually good at assimilating data, are good persuaders, and are objective.

When we think of a perfect organization, we think of a product or service with zero defects; we think of the product or service flowing quickly through our processes with no waste or delay (the seven wastes that form a cornerstone of "lean" thinking); we think of accurate costings and forecasts, real-time information, customers happy with our product or service and wanting to continue to do business with us; continual improvement; good supplier partnerships; a content and stable work-force; a trained workforce; a workforce that suggests improvements to us, and an environment that is the envy of other organizations. Notice anything? Almost all of what has just been described are things that an embedded quality program can help provide and support. Why not use your Quality department in this proactive and strategic way?

Quality and the Management Team

A second area for strategic consideration is the quality of the senior management team. Have desirable characteristics been defined for both individuals and the team? Much has been written on this subject, and at the risk of adding to the considerable literature on the subject, I would like to look at this issue from a different angle.

If we want an integrated management team, I suggest that we look at three levels to achieve a team working in the same direction, with minimal disruption. Succeeding levels will not be effective without the preceding levels being implemented successfully.

> **Level 1:** Self-knowledge (using tools such as the Enneagram and Transactional Analysis). We need to know ourselves, our motivations, our weaknesses, and our strengths. Senior managers should be encouraged, but not forced, to do this kind of self-development.

> **Level 2:** A period of self-development and team development. This will allow people to express doubts and weaknesses within the senior management team without ridicule. Expressing doubts should be seen as coming from a position of strength, where people feel confident enough in themselves and in the team not to feel threatened in saying negative things or asking questions that may either seem trivial or seem to threaten the organization's current view of itself or its environment.

> **Level 3:** A forum for joint problem solving. This helps a team gel while working together on common issues.

It takes more than weekends away or paintball excursions to make a good team. The starting place is self-knowledge and self-improvement, but team building must be done carefully, in a safe environment, and with everyone's agreement. This is probably one reason why it is rarely done. How many people in commercial organizations feel secure enough to admit to shortcomings? For this reason, team building should be done privately, voluntarily, and on a one-to-one basis with a skilled facilitator. Not everyone has the emotional intelligence to go through this, but if done properly, it can have lasting positive effects on individuals and subsequently on the team.

We could run programs such as the Enneagram or Transactional Analysis and inform people that anyone who wants to progress beyond a certain level in the organization will be expected to participate and that participation is for self-development only. Nothing will be shared with their employer.

The outcome of such courses is that senior managers become more aware of their own strengths and weaknesses and develop an appreciation of how other people see them and see the world. This helps them in dealing effectively and meaningfully with other managers and with external stakeholders. If the courses are determined to be useful, participation could be cascaded to the next management level.

As part of their own development and of team building, senior management should consider further training for themselves at monthly group sessions. These training sessions could be run by an internal person (anyone who has the relevant expertise) or by an external trainer. This can provide a great opportunity for someone within the organization to shine. Along with quality related sessions every few months, other training topics could include finance, theory of constrains (TOC), lean, risk management, project management, Microsoft Office software tips, tips on any proprietary software being used, data presentation, risk management tools, internal auditing, social media, the Enneagram, Transactional Analysis, ISO 9001, and basic business and technical vocabulary for various languages. These training sessions can be held on-site or off-site.

If found to be useful, a lot of this training can be cascaded to lower levels. At the end of the day, we want well-trained and integrated management teams at various levels in the organization.

Everyone has shortcomings, weaknesses, things we shy away from, different ways of approaching people and problems, different strengths, different ways of seeing the world, different conflict resolution approaches, different ways of being. Yet because of the traditional macho image in most organizations, this crucial reality is ignored, and everyone pretends that being extroverted is the only way, that they have no doubts, that they don't need help, that situations are under control. This is obviously untrue, so why do we pretend? Why do we reward professional bullies, people who bulldoze their way through meetings and their dealings with people? "Well, he doesn't have the best way of dealing with people, but he gets results." Is this the nub of the issue? Does the end justify the means? It's easy to bully your way through things, because it usually means you don't have to listen. As someone once said, "listening takes courage." Really listening might mean you have to change your own point of view or acknowledge that someone else's idea is better. And this is where bullying negatively affects a profit-making organization. The better ideas get ignored because the boss wants us to go in direction X, or buy company Y. Sometimes these decisions ruin an organization.

We don't need wimps at the top of an organization; all I'm saying is that we should not just assume that the biggest talkers are automatically the best people for the job, and that at all management levels, we should encourage diversity of styles as well as backgrounds. We can tweak our culture and reward system so that, for example, introverts or technical experts have an equal chance of progressing within an organization. This can only happen if the structure is there to support it, and we at least give equal consideration to those who view things differently or express themselves differently.

For example, introverts often need time to reflect on new data, so asking for an immediate reaction or decision does not work well for them. We should ask introverted people to come back with a response within a certain time period.

Is our organization mature enough to recognize the differences in people and not see those differences as weaknesses? Do we as senior managers really listen to others?

CHAPTER SUMMARY

In this chapter we looked at strategy and at how Quality could be incorporated into strategic thinking and strategic plans. We spoke about how Porter's model of competitive forces could be tailored to include Quality, and finally we looked at how we might assess and improve the quality of the management team.

Questions

1. Have you clearly explained your organization's strategy to all departments? This usually means more than just an email or a report.

2. Have you explicitly asked your Quality director or Quality manager to identify ways that their department can contribute to the organization's strategy?

3. Do you invite the Quality director to the strategy meetings?

4. Has any of your team done a self-development course?

5. How do you promote diversity in your organization and in decision making?

CHAPTER THREE

***

Quality Culture

CHAPTER OUTLINE:

In this chapter, we consider the importance of attitude in achieving quality throughout an organization, and we discuss tried and tested methods of employee involvement such as suggestion schemes and relevant training. This chapter also proposes that quality objectives should be explicit in every manager's KPIs and annual appraisal.

When I speak of culture, I refer to the values, attitudes, beliefs, and customs of an organization—how things are done in an organization.

To change a culture, we, as senior managers, must be on-board. Only then will the proper support mechanisms be in place.

People, according to Daniel Pink in his book *Drive*, want autonomy, mastery, and purpose (AMP) in their work. Is that not something we can all identify with, when we think of our own jobs? If AMP applies to us in our roles, why should it not apply to others, at whatever level they are in the organization? And if we believe this, then we need to seriously look again at how work is organized. (There is an interesting cartoon-type video of the AMP theory on YouTube, at www.youtube.com/watch?feature=player_embedded&v=u6XAPnuFjJc). When it comes to dealing with the ground troops in an organization, we seem obsessed with controlling and measuring them. We introduce monitoring systems and we make shop floor personnel refer to work instructions for tasks they are doing five days a week. But let's turn our viewpoint around. Do I want my boss micromanaging me like that? I doubt if any manager wants that, but the reality is that *nobody* wants that. We create whole systems to control people, but what is wrong with training people, giving each group a cell leader (to be chosen by the group or the managers), and saying words to the effect of: "here is the output we need (e.g., x widgets, or y transactions). As long as we get this, we won't be interfering. We will provide support (equipment maintenance, IT support, Quality support, Health and Safety support, training). Let us know if you need anything else or if there is a risk that you will not meet this target."

Would we be prepared to do this? Isn't this similar, in the broad sense, to how we ourselves are managed? Would we be prepared to try this in one section of our organization?

An attitude of continual improvement is the key to improving our business. We need to have a culture where people are not afraid to suggest changes, and where such suggestions are recognized and rewarded. When we ask that question of our own organization, can we honestly say that this is in place, or is it just in a policy somewhere, just a soundbite, but not implemented? How do we encourage improvement in our own organizations? I have been in organizations where this philosophy was quoted, but in meetings, new or different ideas were shot down very quickly.

Any organization proposing to go down the route of encouraging suggestions should look at the end point first. What will we do with these suggestions; how will they be evaluated; who will evaluate them; what do we do about suggestions that are unworkable, impractical, too expensive, or malicious; and how, or will we, reward people for suggestions we decide to implement? There is nothing more demotivating than to introduce a suggestion scheme and then ignore the suggestions and this must be avoided at all costs—it is better to not start a suggestion scheme than to start one and do it half-heartedly.

Another way to solicit suggestions is to do it in real time through supervisor or manager conversations with employees. This can reduce the administrative effort involved with a suggestion scheme or suggestion board, but success depends heavily on the quality of the individual supervisor or manager. If they are not open to new ideas or think it is only they who should be suggesting things, this approach will not work well. The conversations should focus on asking employees what waste they see, what is stopping them from achieving better results, what issues they have with the internal or external suppliers, etc.

Also useful is the ABC approach to managing people, which suggests that attitude leads to behavior, which has consequences (good and bad). Again, this emphasizes the importance of attitude. But how often do we specifically look for this attitude when interviewing people? Even before that stage, do we know what attitudes we want? We focus more on education, experience, and qualifications because these are usually more quantifiable and more measureable. Candidates' attitudes should be assessed at the interview stage, because we must ensure that people are the right fit for our organization. This is even more important, in some respects, than the candidate's qualifications, because people can always be taught the skills the job requires; it is much more difficult to change someone's attitude. There are plenty of people with similar skills for most jobs. A person's unique selling point (USP) is attitude and the mix of influences that make them who and what they are and how they perform. I suggest the senior management team spend time (perhaps with the help of an outside facilitator or expert) determining the core attitudes we want in our prospective employees.

Motivation is key to encouraging people to do a job right. Some of the standard methods of trying to motivate people include:

- Being and feeling respected and appreciated by their manager
- Having opportunities to learn
- Having opportunities for increased responsibilities
- Being trusted to make decisions—having authority and resources
- Being given recognition for a job well done—even a "thank you"
- Being given a reward such as a voucher, a small cash reward, flex time, a day off, or prizes for a team/department get together (ask staff what they would like)
- Inviting a coach or motivational speaker
- Asking them to benchmark a product against a competitor's
- Giving people autonomy, mastery, and purpose (AMP) in their jobs
- Seeing their recommendations adopted
- Overseeing a job through from start to finish

Why not consider using the annual appraisal of managers and staff to include quality elements such as these:

- The number of quality audits done or where assistance was given (minimum of one per quarter)—even getting managers to accompany an auditor can be enlightening for the manager.
- The number of repeat non-conformances relating to their sphere of authority and responsibility.
- The amount of quality related training done.
- The number of quality or performance enhancements/ suggestions made to their process;
- The number of preventive actions implemented.
- A look at the department's or organization's level of risk compared to a year ago.

- Ensuring that business risk assessments, quality plans, procedures, work instructions, and other controlled documents are reviewed at least once per year and updated as required and after complaints, market feedback, external environment feedback, process changes, design changes, material or supplier changes, and audit reports (both internal and external).

- The number of issues they resolved and owned (even if the cause was not due to their department). Good managers should be looking beyond the boundaries of their own departments.

There are several ways to encourage new ideas for promoting quality: setting up teams for the best quality innovation or quality enhancement and encouraging internal competition for the biggest reduction in waste or variation, or increased production, or most money saved. These do not cost much to set up or reward. Why not try it in one area or on one site? You can add specific boundaries to the trial in terms of time period and reward.

Be sure rewards are something people actually want. How far does a coffee mug or a free pizza go in motivating someone? Rewards should mean something to prospective recipients, and there should be a choice. Rewards can include free training; a free weekend trip; visits to suppliers or customers; time off to pursue something that, while not part of their job, could benefit the organization; an opportunity to present their ideas to senior management (employees invariably have ideas that could save time or effort); or a paid day off.

What are the implications for managers if they are to be made explicitly responsible for quality, environmental safety, H&S, and CSR (corporate social responsibility) in their respective areas? How would their roles and their training change? What KPIs should be added to their performance metrics? Is this not a way of getting more meaningful action on these issues? People will take action where a KPI exists for it (as long as we are conscious of the metric pitfalls that are discussed elsewhere in this book).

Although it has no direct impact on quality, organizations should consider adopting a charity or local community group and encourage employees to help out (clean up a local area, raise funds...). This can boost morale and enhance the organization's standing in the community. It also sends a positive culture signal within the organization.

Senior managers can encourage change and promote quality by:

- Accompanying someone who is doing a quality audit.
- Being seen in the work areas more. This has elements of management by walking around (MBWA), but it can be a sign of positive reinforcement.

- Accompanying someone who is doing a supplier audit.
- Being present when a customer or certification body is auditing your organization.
- Involving people.
- Training people.
- Leading by example.
- Ensuring that the Quality department is seen as helping the other departments.
- Explaining the objectives.
- Integrating quality into all aspects of the organization, into all processes and activities.
- Showing the benefits—saving time, money, and reduced frustration with the system.
- Promoting the best people to or from the Quality department.
- Using the organization newsletter by developing a with a quality quiz or quality crossword.
- Making everyone aware that the system is there to help. People should not be afraid to ask for changes to the system to help them in their work.

Senior managers have a pivotal role in deciding the culture of an organization. You can tell if you have it wrong by looking at things like these:

- The number of people leaving (when the market is buoyant);
- People rebelling in small ways by resisting, going slow, making excuses, retiring on the job
- A blame culture
- Managers focussing on their budgets instead of the performance of the organization (e.g., wanting to charge other departments for 15 minutes work)

Metrics must be discussed by those involved, and we should actively consider reasons why they might not work, might not give the desired result, or might give the wrong results. Only after this discussion should we go ahead and implement metrics.

"What gets measured, gets done; what gets rewarded, gets repeated."
– attributed to various business writers

Why should we think that the people on the ground floor are any different from those at the top? They might (or might not) have less education, less money, or less experience, but as people they are not different (and they can sometimes have *more* education or experience than those at the top). They have experiences and skills that are important to the effective and efficient running of our organization. If we want to be the best, we should not assume that management are the only ones with answers to problems facing the organization. We may already have cross functional teams, but sometimes it can be hard for those at the lower level of an organization to get their voices heard, so we could consider ideas like these:

- When significant changes are being proposed, set up a forum where anyone can make suggestions that will improve the change or highlight weaknesses in the proposal.

- Have a regular forum for various departments, where anyone can make suggestions.

- Consider a suggestion box. These have had bad press, usually because they are not used properly. Managers either don't read the suggestions, ignore them, or fail to give feedback. The whole thing can be too secretive. If you decide to use suggestion cards, the following rules should apply:

  - The card should allow the person to indicate whether they wish to be identified and whether they wish the suggestion to be publicized. Some may prefer to retain anonymity, especially if they are pointing out shortcomings in existing practices. In this regard, it is useful to have a whistle-blower policy.

  - There should be meaningful rewards for suggestions that are adopted.

  - All cards must be reviewed not only by the relevant manager, but by at least two other people, perhaps one from HR and a senior manager.

  - Feedback is crucial to a successful suggestion box scheme, so a commitment must be given by the organization to give an initial response within, say, five working days.

  - Some organizations have a board where all suggestions, responses, and actions are noted, but I think this should not be mandatory for all suggestions.

Forums can be a great way of spotting hidden talent in an organization and can be a great way to encourage the cross-fertilization of ideas. The forums must be attended by more than one manager, and preferably should include at least one senior manager. These can be a great learning experience for the managers because they get to hear some of the real issues at the coalface, as well as fresh ideas to tackle issues facing the organization. Senior managers can take turns attending these forums to ensure that any feedback to the top table is not just the view of one person. Forums can be created for many areas, such as a product or product family, a department, an investment proposal, a "new ideas" program, a cost reduction plan, etc.

We could do worse than refer to Mintzberg's theory of motivation regarding hygiene and motivating factors.

- Hygiene factors—healthcare benefits, vacation days, pay, working conditions

- Motivating factors—recognition, pride, sense of achievement, authority, responsibility, workmanship, ownership

Hygiene factors keep people ticking over and may motivate someone for a short period, but they will not achieve much more than that. For motivation, we need to look at other factors. There are plenty of books and resources online that explain the theory in more detail.

The key skills of a good senior manager include balancing the competing interests of different departments and people (from both inside and outside the organization), focusing on the external environment, and devising and implementing an integrated and coherent strategy. Good executives are good people managers; they quickly understand the critical few issues versus the trivial many; they are decisive in evaluating risks; and they can rephrase situations to make the choices and consequences clearer.

Senior management must ask the "so what" questions. Why are data being collected and what will be done as a result of having that data? If there are no good answers to these fundamental questions, then it's time to find more meaningful metrics. A more fundamental question for senior management might be this. Are we only managing by metrics? Metrics do not give the whole story; they do not give us insight into the morale of the employees, nor do they show resentment or hostility that might exist between departments or between managers. These are issues that can sap the energy from an organization and encourage the creation of silos.

If we as senior management are really serious about our commitment to Quality, then we should be demonstrating that we want only good quality product or a good service going to customers, even if that means stopping or delaying shipments or services or recalling product. This is a brave step to take, yet it can make financial sense. Sometimes senior management fails to be rigorous in its thinking, fails to take the step back, and fails to resolve the perennial issue. We put undue pressure on production or service personnel to "get the stuff out the door within the deadline, no matter what," and we put undue pressure on the Quality department to "let it ship." This is just management by metrics, not real management. It is a mentality that equates quantity shipped with good management.

Many organizations are run by metrics; people do need to meet their objectives and targets. Should the same logic apply to specifications? Most products (and many services) have specifications and tolerances (or service level agreements). The product or service is either in or out of specification. This seems clear and simple, but in the real world there are always other factors at play, such as:

- Cosmetic specifications, which often cannot cover every possible cosmetic issue that could arise;

- Defects that are known to the organization but will not affect the form, fit, or function of the product;

- The pressure to meet production targets; and

- Delays in providing the specified service where those delays may not be critical to the customer.

I contend that it is counterproductive to give the Quality department sole responsibility as gatekeeper for the organization. We tell the quality manager, "You're responsible if any bad product ships out or our service falls below expectations," or words to that effect. The first problem with this approach is that responsibility has moved, from the department responsible, to QA. The second problem is one of trust. We don't trust our own production people to make the correct decision. Have we ever stopped to look at how our own behavior as senior managers contributes to this situation? Do we trust our own ability to do our jobs right? Do we trust our direct reports to do their job right? We can cascade this thinking down the organization. But where does it break down, where do we stop trusting, and just as importantly, why?

If I, as a senior manager, tell the operations manager and production manager and service manager that they will be measured equally on delivery and quality, should they not be then ensuring that only good products leave the factory or that compliant services are delivered? If managers are told that any product returned or reported service fault will be deducted from their shipping figures, or that x% of the value of any returns will be deducted from their bonus or will result in a % decrease in any pay rise, will they not change their behavior and change how inspection is performed and how products or services are checked?

Now let us just hold things there for a moment, and look at the potential unintended consequences of this approach. It is right that operations/production/service managers should be explicitly told that they are also responsible for the quality of what they produce, but we need to be careful of reducing someone's bonus or pay increase. This can end up producing the wrong behavior. People will start hiding problems, or worse, will get into an argument with QA every time there is an issue, because they don't want it impacting their income. This is where senior management must be clear in its objectives for departmental managers. How do we prevent the hiding of issues or argument situations from arising? If we have cascaded the top-level objectives properly, we should have already looked at the law of unintended consequences and tweaked the lower level objectives accordingly.

Senior managers are responsible for ensuring that there is a culture of only good product leaving the premises, and that every department is on the same side. All too often there is the quality versus production argument, and even after all this time, the battle rages on.

> *How much more effective would organizations be, if the production and Quality departments were perfectly aligned, striving for the same goal—that only good product will be delivered to customers?*

The message in the box above is simple to say, but most organizations seem unable or unwilling to get to that stage. Instead, they prefer to have continual battles between departments; to carry the costs of scrap, rework, returned product, and non-value-added inspection costs; and to lose good people who are frustrated with the structure and culture. This makes no sense, yet we senior managers have allowed this to develop. It is not usually a conscious decision; rather, it results from failing to question why things are the way they are and put a plan in place to stop it.

The better approach is to reward managers for resolving issues with effective corrective action, for reducing the number of issues, and for preventing issues repeating. In this way, we move from the "deduction in your salary" approach to a "chance to increase your salary" approach. We don't actively penalize people when something goes wrong (unless it is deliberate), we incentivize people for doing a better job. This is the win-win situation we want and the incentive need not always be money.

If people are of a quality mindset, if the organization supports that and allows people to be objective about their own and other people's work, why shouldn't production carry out inspection? Why don't we create a system that allows people doing the work to know whether what they have done is of good quality? We need to offer training and create an environment where people can do this properly, knowing that they will not be criticized for rejecting bad product.

Is senior management really serious about its commitment to quality? What if the answer is "no"? What if a departmental or senior manager is not onside about the Quality ethos or has a negative attitude to quality? What are the steps we can take to resolve this? We can try the following:

1. We can meet with managers to understand their position and why they hold that view. The function of this meeting is to listen. Only by listening will we get an understanding of where they are and thus be able to come up with a roadmap to help them move from where they are now to where the organization needs them to be. We need to be aware that they may have valid reasons for holding their view.

2. We need to show the failings of the current system, to show how it reduces efficiency and effectiveness and increases costs. But facts and figures may not be enough. We must also remember that we did not arrive at our changed attitude to quality overnight; it is reasonable to allow others time to make that mental journey. Changing how someone thinks about a long-held view is not simple. We need to allow time, but showing the problems and costs of the current situation can be a powerful tool in promoting change. It's also important to consider the estimated costs of doing nothing.

3. If we have examples of where the new system is working, it is worthwhile to let the reluctant managers talk with those who have been involved with that change.

4. We can also review other tools and techniques listed in the chapter on change management.

When we look behind the presented causes of bad quality, we often see other deeper causes, but for the purposes of this discussion, I am only focussing on the people side of things:

- Lack of motivation/interest, fear, stress
- Shortage of people
- Lack of training/skills
- Unqualified personnel
- People taking shortcuts

These issues are related to people and culture and are the responsibility of us as senior managers. If they can be addressed over time, an organization will be well on its way to becoming a top performer. If we believe in our employees and their desire to do a good job, we need to free them of the restrictions within organizations to reap the benefits.

CHAPTER SUMMARY

In this chapter, we looked at the relationship between quality and attitude and at the criticality of including explicit quality related objectives in every manager's KPIs and appraisal. We asked why production and quality goals are not aligned, and we touched on the fundamentally flawed notion that quality managers are responsible for quality. We ended by looking at why it's important to hold senior managers responsible for "people" issues.

Questions

1. How do you encourage or reward people for doing a good job?
2. How do you encourage improvement?
3. Do you have any counterproductive or conflicting metrics?
4. Do you have quality objectives in every manager's objectives?
5. Are you over-focused on metrics, to the detriment of good management and common sense?

CHAPTER FOUR

✳ ✳ ✳

Quality and Customers

CHAPTER OUTLINE:

In this chapter we look at determining customer requirements, whether explicit or implicit, we introduce the concept of the internal customer, and we look at customer contracts from a quality metrics viewpoint.

In discussing customers, it is clear that a lot depends on the type of product we make or the service we provide. Is it an off-the-shelf item or custom made? Is it a hardware or software product? Is it a bespoke service? Is it a franchise service?

It's also important to consider whether we sell direct to a consumer, through a distributor, to other businesses, or through a combination of some or all of these. Each of these affects every aspect of how we deal with customers and each of these three types of customers has different expectations. Needless to say, there can be cultural implications also, so we need to be familiar with local markets.

We often start with market research, because it's important to first determine what the customer wants or needs and then look at how our product or service can satisfy those wants and needs. We also need to ensure that our processes can meet customer requirements. Many organizations are afraid to say "no" to a customer or to a customer-specific requirement, and this can result in a product or service that will never make a profit for us. This is not usually a black and white situation. Often organizations knowingly accept a loss-making contract in the expectation of getting more lucrative work from that customer later. Sometimes that expectation is more correctly described as hope, when the customer has not given any indication that they *will* grant us more business. Another common approach is to hold the initial purchase price artificially low in order to win the contract or business and then try to claw back the money by means of product revisions, service changes and enhancements, or costly maintenance contracts. Senior management needs to be dispassionate about how these decisions are made. It might look great to do work for a well-respected or large customer, but is it financially sustainable over several years? There can be downsides to this approach. Examples include:

- We find ourselves responding to the whims of a customer that represents such a large proportion of our business. We offer special deals, hold extra stock, loan one of our people to the customer's design team, or offer free delivery.

- Customers place unrealistic demands on us in terms of selling price, lead times, 24/7 support, and so on. Things like packaging or transport requirements can force us into making large capital purchases or incurring ongoing costs that were not included in the original project evaluation.

- Large customers can require a high level of product specialization or a particular combination of options, both of which could be very difficult to deliver consistently.

- In the retail sector, some customers require suppliers to pay a stocking fee, which can destroy a small organization's profitability.

The message is that the dream contract might not be as lucrative as first thought. Suppliers must know about the things that can jeopardize profitability and should prepare a checklist of issues to consider before pursuing that business, in fact, anything that might result in more time and money needed to supply products or deliver a service. This checklist should be fully reviewed before accepting a large contract. We might still accept the contract, but at least we accept it knowing the potential pitfalls, and we can set up a monitor to alert us of the key risks identified.

The items mentioned previously in relation to how we might make a contract ultimately profitable are all assumptions; there is no guarantee that some or any of these will actually happen. We need to consider what we can or will do if these assumptions do not become reality, and ask about the foundations of such assumptions. On what are they based? This is why we need to regularly monitor financial performance in relation to each contract, so that we can decide whether corrective action is required.

I worked with an organization where we got a lucrative contract. We assumed certain productivity efficiencies that never materialized. Because of this, we ended up having to work a lot of night and weekend overtime, and having to fly product to the customer. Result—we were stuck in a contract while hemorrhaging money.

As customer requirements change over time, and perhaps in shorter timeframes than previously, we need to periodically revisit our product or service offering to ensure it still meets the needs of the market. Where this results in a new product or service, then Quality personnel can have a role to play in ensuring that both product or service and also support systems are configured to maximize efficiency, minimize waste or duplication, and continually meet requirements. This includes working with R&D to look at ways to design out weaknesses from older products or services or previous versions of products or services (i.e., ensuring we have an effective "lessons learned" process).

Customer wants and needs

- Do we know what they are, especially the critical-to-quality (CTQ) wants and needs?

- How do we know their wants and needs? Does information come from an objective source?

- Are these requirements measurable? If so, have we metrics in place to measure our performance against and alignment with these requirements?

- Do we ask customers for feedback on our performance? Is negative feedback filtered before it reaches senior management?

- How often do we review customer wants and needs?

- When we draw up a project/product/service costing, do we perform scenario planning to see how the ROI is affected by various internal and external factors?

- Is there a limit to how far we should customize our product or service to suit individual customers? If so, is that limit defined?

- How do we try to embed ourselves with our customers?

- What is our relationship with our customers? Are we helpful, confrontational, submissive?

If we are producing a product or service that is similar to something already in the market, we might be able to strip down a competitor's offering. This benchmarking approach can give us an insight into the competition and show us possible improvements, but used on its own benchmarking will rarely enable us to be best in class; it generally takes no account of innovation.

Where we are introducing a new product, it can be hard to get information about customer requirements, and this is where sales or marketing people can be a big help. They should be going to customers and asking these questions:

- What would make this product or service better from your point of view?
- Are there features missing?
- What does this product or service *not* have that others have?
- Do you think this product or service represents good value to you?

These are key questions, and answers need to be fed back to the design department and to senior management. Ultimately it is up to senior management to decide what to do about this feedback.

Other ways of getting useful customer information are customer metrics (where a customer provides monthly or quarterly feedback) and customer surveys, although surveys often have a very low response rate. It is usually far more productive for Sales or Marketing or account management people to directly talk to customers when they visit.

It is important that we identify the CTQ items in the product or service *from the customer's point of view*. This is key information that should be fed back to the R&D, Quality, and manufacturing departments and to the service providers.

Many organizations now use online surveys and online customer feedback. These are generally very easy to set up and manage, but often there is insufficient thought given to determining the purpose of the survey. What information do we want and what are we planning to do with that information? Most of us have completed online surveys that were missing options or comment sections, or that had options that were too restrictive. If we do a survey, let us at least plan it and implement it well. We should trial it on some of our employees or on one or two customers before releasing it online.

Because surveys can have a poor response rate, we should consider giving money off the next purchase, putting responders into a drawing, or promising a charitable donation for every response received.

Other questions we can ask ourselves and our existing customers include those shown in Figure 5.

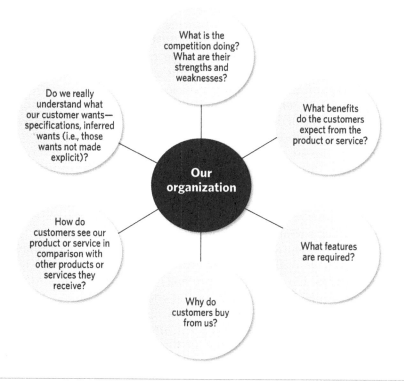

Figure 5   Organization vision.

Questions for senior management include:

- Are we customer focused?
- Do we listen to customers? Do we know what problems they have?
- Are we on the customer's side?
- Do we show how customers could gain a competitive advantage from using our product or service?
- Do we suggest features the customer could use or benefit from? Our thinking should be, how can what I provide help their problem or business?
- What are the repeating issues or complaints? What are the trends? Is there a Pareto diagram of the returns? These are simple ways to ensure we focus on the important issues.

Once we have established that there is a need for our product or service and we have decided to provide it, we must look at how this is translated internally. For certain industries, there might be a user requirement specification, which can be a useful and formal way of defining exactly what the customer wants and expects.

Most manufacturing industries use drawings and specifications, either generated internally or supplied by the customer. These drawings may include specific areas marked "special characteristics" or "critical-to-quality" characteristics. These help focus where extra controls are required by the supplier. These critical areas may require verification or validation or capability studies to demonstrate (to ourselves and the customer) that our processes are capable of consistently producing product within the specification. We must satisfy ourselves that we can make the product consistently and that we can achieve the requirements and assumptions related to the contract.

The pharmaceutical, automotive, and medical device industries (and others) have well established processes for covering these elements through things like advanced product quality planning (APQP) or installation qualification (IQ), operational qualification (OQ), and performance qualification (PQ) processes.

CTQ features can, of course, be also applied to the service sector. It's just a question of identifying what are the key transactions in the service provision process.

It's important that we understand internal and external customer needs. An internal customer may be another department within our organization, other branches, or other steps in our process. Design departments should be conscious of their internal customers in terms of "design for manufacture" and "design for assembly." The external customer focus is on the end user and logistics. How will the parts be packaged, labelled, loaded, transported, used, serviced, disposed of, decommissioned, or recycled? This is where product life cycle analysis comes into play, and this is an area that will become more important in the future. We can already see consumers want to know how "green" products are, and how much CO_2 is used in transporting goods from where they are made or grown (the carbon footprint). Associated with this is the whole area of corporate responsibility and ethics, so it is easy to see that we need to consider a wider range of issues than just "how cheap can we make this product or design this service?"

Of course, we can choose to ignore all of these "soft" issues, but analyzing these factors can be a source of competitive advantage and may give us access to certain customers from which we might otherwise be excluded.

We should be encouraging more than only Sales or Marketing or account managers to visit customers. Why not ask representatives from Quality, Engineering, Purchasing, or Operations to visit? It can only be beneficial for these people to see how the final product or service is used and how what *they* do contributes to this.

The corollary of this is to invite customers to your organization. Usually this only happens when a customer is auditing a supplier, or a new product or service is being discussed, but why not encourage other visits? There can be several benefits:

- It can help the customer to see the problems that a supplier has with a customer-designed product because of a design weakness.

- It helps develop and strengthen the relationship between supplier and customer.

- It can be motivational to the workforce when a customer is interested enough to visit a supplier and talk to employees.

- It can help uncover duplication between supplier systems or documents and those of a customer.

- It can encourage a relationship of trust, which can help current and future business.

- It allows other departments to interact. We often invite customer purchasing or supplier quality personnel; why not invite some of the employees who actually use our product or service? Having actual users meet actual product makers or service providers could spark an interesting discussion.

Repeat business depends more on trust and good relationships with key people than on relying solely on product quality, service quality, or price. People buy from people.

Many medium- to large-volume orders, or orders that have a high value or a long duration, have contracts associated with them. These contracts are often based on a standard format, and many template versions are available online. Most organizations probably have similar contracts, and these can be tweaked to suit new customers or products or services. However, existing contracts may contain references to previous customers or products/services. Proofreading of previously-used contracts is crucial.

From a quality point of view, contracts usually specify basic information:

1. The quality target that must be achieved. This might be an actual number, a percentage, parts per million (PPM), parts per billion (PPB), "number of defects per x parts delivered," or something similar. In a later chapter, we will look at the disadvantages of using some of these metrics and suggest an alternative approach. Contracts may also categorize the defects into major and minor (or critical, major, and minor), with different numerical targets for each.

2. Limit samples that are agreed to between the two organizations. These are samples representing the extremes of what is acceptable in terms of color, dimensions, strength, performance, etc., but can also include service-related factors (see item 9).

3. Reference samples. If the supplier and customer have identical samples, then it should minimize disagreement about whether a part is acceptable or not.

4. Delivery performance.

5. How complaints are handled and any associated costs.

6. How parts are labelled and packaged (and possibly transported).

7. The responsibilities of the supplier when something goes wrong.

8. The liabilities of the supplier.

9. A service level agreement (SLA). For service organizations, the standard contract will define the frequency of visits (where the service involves visiting client sites), what is done at each visit, who is responsible if access to a customer site is not possible, what records are to be supplied to the customer, and what happens if a visit is missed by the supplier. For other services, the SLA might cover the turnaround time of a query, the number of calls made, the percentage of issues resolved by the first contact person, the percentage of repeat customers, etc.

10. The duration of support for non-current product. This includes the length of time support will be offered, or the availability of spare parts for obsolete product. This can affect how much old tooling, parts, and space must set aside to support old products.

We will consider further details of what should go into contracts when we look at suppliers, and we should always compare customer contracts with those we generate for suppliers; they are really two sides of the same coin.

CHAPTER SUMMARY

In this chapter we looked at different ways to determine customer wants/needs/requirements. We also spoke about the importance of the internal customer. One senior management responsibility is to ensure a smooth flow of information, product, and process between all departments. Lastly, we looked at some items that a Quality department might expect to see in a customer contract.

Questions

1. How well do you know what customers require? How often do you check?

2. What are the underlying assumptions in your costings?

3. Have any of your customer contracts undergone a change to any terms and conditions? If so, have you re-visited the ROI or payback period?

4. When you draw up a project costing, do you include scenario planning? What happens if the exchange rate goes against you, or inflation goes up, or wages increase, or fuel costs increase, or environmental or regulatory requirements change?

5. How do you go about getting the optimum fit between what you provide and what your customer wants?

6. Do all employees know what customers consider the critical features?

7. How do you actively try to embed your organization with your key customers?

8. What is your relationship with your customers? Do you try to help them or do you try to get as much money out of them for as little effort as possible?

CHAPTER FIVE

*** *** ***

Quality and Organization Objectives

CHAPTER OUTLINE:

In this chapter, we look at how objectives derive from an organization's mission and vision, and we look at some top-level objectives. We discuss the negative aspects that are identified when organizations start looking inward rather than outward and we talk about the problem of short-term focus. We introduce the idea that a Quality department must sell its contribution to management in terms of cost saving and integrating quality into an organization. We then look at data-driven decision making and the idea of quality being everyone's responsibility. Finally, I include Dr. W. Edwards Deming's famous 14 points for management. These have become a cornerstone for many Quality people. Even if we don't agree with all of them, they are a great starting point for debate among senior management.

A typical flow chart for an organization's vision, how this cascades through the different levels, and where Quality usually fits is illustrated in Figure 6.

From a senior manager's point of view, it is critical that the organization's objectives (and the Quality objectives) be cascaded so that there is alignment between each department's objectives and the organization's strategic objectives. This must be visible to everyone and senior management must lead by example. Do we, as senior managers, reward appropriate behavior? Have the senior management team explained the organization's strategy to all departments? This needs more than a generic Email. Ideally, small group meetings allow for clarity and feedback.

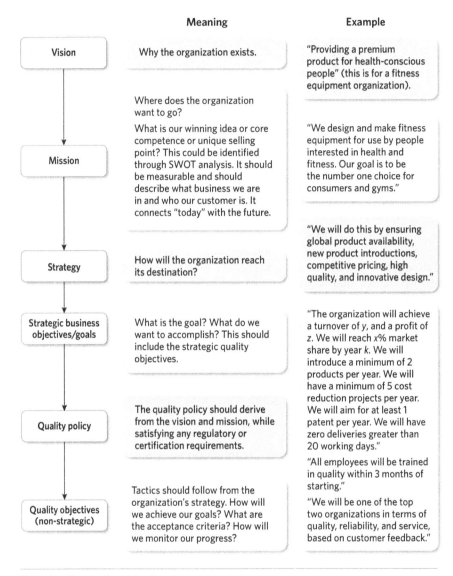

Figure 6   Organization vision flowchart.

Top-level objectives typically include many of the following:

- Make money; improve profitability, improve margins
- Increase throughput
- Increase sales
- Satisfy customers and generate repeat customers

- Increase market share
- Produce excellent quality products or service
- Develop and introduce new products or services
- Look for new markets for existing products or services
- Reduce costs, reduce waste, reduce activities that do not add value
- Maximize resource use
- Be a safe place to work
- Minimize any pollution of the environment
- Support the local community
- Encourage diversity
- Operate ethically

Once the high-level objectives have been defined, identify the key steps required to achieve them. This is often done using the SMART goal-setting framework. Without measurable goals with monitoring in place, we would have only aspirations. Senior managers must realize that deciding who is involved in identifying and working on these key steps goes a long way to defining the organization's culture. Will we include only regional managers or plant managers, or will we invite lower-level managers and/or non-managers to also be involved?

A related key question to ask ourselves is this. How do we demonstrate and communicate the above objectives to everyone in the organization? We could do this in several ways:

- Through group meetings.
- By making it part of the induction process.
- By including them in the employee booklet.
- By using the home page of the organization's intranet.
- By ensuring that the relevant objectives are reflected in everyone's individual objectives.

Relevant objectives are objectives that an employee can affect. It is demoralizing and wasteful to give employees objectives they cannot affect. I have seen organizations where, with the best of intentions, it was decided that all the high-level objectives would be in everyone's individual objectives. But I fail to see the benefit of putting "increase market share by 3%" into the objectives of a shop floor worker. There are relevant and meaningful objectives that contribute to achieving the same overall goal but mean more to the individual employee.

In relation to Quality specifically, have we as senior managers ever asked (and answered) this question? How do people in the organization know that Quality is important to senior management? Where is the evidence for this? Have we ever asked our employees?

When devising a vision, mission, strategy, policy, goals, or objectives it can be helpful to use the "SEEQS" approach (Table 2). This allows senior managers to be conscious of these areas when formulating the various policies. It might be something as simple as using the following table as a tick box. For each tick, we need to add notes showing *how* we determined that a tick was applicable and what is or will be the evidence or record to prove it. This can then be added as a metric so that it will be monitored and acted upon.

From reading business magazines and listening to business news, one could get the impression that many organizations have lost customer focus and have become inwardly focused.

An inward focus is evidenced by things like:

- Success is measured by the volume shipped, not by the volume of *good* product shipped.

- Directors and managers are allowed to structure the organization so that they can build an empire and reward themselves. We have seen large organizations buy or merge with other organizations, only to break up a few years later, often at a huge loss. Then someone else takes over and the process of M&A followed by demerger starts again.

Table 2 SEEQS approach.

	Safe	Ethical	Environmentally Friendly	Ensures Quality	Sustainable
Vision					
Mission					
Strategy					
Strategic Objectives					
Policies—Quality, Safety, IT, Email, etc.					
Departmental or Geographic Objectives					

- Within the arena of quality, metrics such as parts per million (PPM), percentage of complaints, or defects per million opportunities (DPMO) are used. Not only do these metrics "allow" us to ship a certain amount of defect product as a function of the volume shipped, but their focus is that of the organization, not of the customer. Customers do not care how much we ship; they only want to know that all the product or service they bought from us is of good quality.

- Incentives are offered for higher sales or cost reductions irrespective of the effect on employees or customers.

Sometimes this inward focus is caused by short-term pressure from investors or the stock market. This can result in directors having a short-term focus, which may not be to the long-term benefit of the organization. Directors and managers must take a step back and understand their basic function in an organization. Are they there to run the organization for the benefit of their investors, their employees, their customers, the government, society, or themselves? Or is it all of these? If it is all of these, then the job of senior management is to balance the conflicting requirements of all stakeholders.

In my view, directors and managers have an obligation to convince investors that by focussing on longer-term goals, they will generate longer-term revenue streams, keep the organization operating profitably, and produce better returns over time (assuming that the business has a long-term future). This includes showing where investment is needed, quantifying that investment, and evaluating that investment (e.g., payback period, return on investment).

The relatively frequent movement of CEOs (and other senior managers) between large organizations means that these CEOs are often not there to see the result of the policies they introduce, yet the effects of these policies can last a long time.

> *Incentives drive the wrong behavior because they focus on those receiving the bonus instead of on the customer.*
> **– Tripp Babbitt**

Do our organizational objectives include those we have obtained directly from our customers? Have we attempted to elicit feedback from customers—by means of surveys, focus group, benchmarking, interviews, workshops, seminars—and used these as inputs to our objectives?

There is no reason why capitalism cannot have a moral side. It is possible to do what's best for the long-term interests of the organization and maximize profit while at the same time ensuring that people are not disadvantaged through unnecessary redundancies, injuries at work, or dangerous products that appear on the market. This doesn't mean ignoring the realities of the bottom line; it just means recognizing that there are other things to consider.

A note on objectives

It's important to set objectives carefully to avoid unintended consequences. We hear about these situations every week—hospitals manipulating waiting times, governments changing how unemployment figures are calculated, schools falsifying results, car emission scandals. We create KPIs that we deem untouchable, but people will ways try to find a way around them in order to make themselves look good. This is human nature. This is why we must be careful of conflicting KPIs. It would be a disaster to end up with a culture where people avoid, ignore, or cover up issues because of the effect on their KPI (and resulting bonus or appraisal). Once this mentality takes hold, senior managers can end up receiving signals that everything is fine when the reality is very different. How do we prevent this situation from developing? How do we ensure that, although people need to be held accountable for their actions, we don't just blame and punish those who appear to have made a mistake? If someone does something illegal or commits fraud, that is a separate issue, but usually it is our systems that result in mistakes—we make things too complicated, we don't provide enough training, we don't provide adequate resources, or we impose unrealistic deadlines. Are we sure none of these apply (at management level) before we start blaming an employee?

It's important not rely excessively on metrics because this can result in demotivation. Running an organization by metrics will rarely result in outstanding performance, and over-reliance on metrics can create a bureaucratic organization. It is also an example of an inward-looking organization, where managers are satisfied (and rewarded accordingly) as long as the results meet the KPIs. Most KPIs have no customer focus, and even those that do are subject to manipulation. It's not that KPIs are always a bad thing, but I would suggest we need far fewer. We need to anticipate unintended consequences before introducing KPIs, and we should create them from the customer's viewpoint—either the external or internal customer.

Serving customers and meeting their needs is a means to the end of making money. When push comes to shove, organizations usually focus on money—how to make more (by increasing sales volume or increasing the sales price) or how to reduce costs.

Are our KPIs inward-looking? How many of our KPIs are customer-focused?

> *I have experienced situations where a KPI was to have as few complaints as possible. Department heads spent an extraordinary amount of time and effort trying to prove that a complaint wasn't really a complaint and shouldn't be counted in their metric. The focus was not on eliminating problems but on how to deflect the issue. This is a classic example of the pitfalls of trying to run an organization using KPIs.*

How can we achieve the primary goal of making money by satisfying customers at a profit?

There are a number of ways:

- Increase sales volume: This usually involves selling more to existing customers, or selling the same products to new customers, or perhaps buying a competitor.

- Increase sales price: This will usually work only if we do not supply a commodity and if our strategy is not that of lowest-cost producer. Often the strategy involves adding new features (differentiation) or re-launching or re-branding a product.

- Reduce costs: We can reduce costs by moving to a low-cost manufacturing location; by reducing waste (using approaches such as lean management, the TIMWOOD mnemonic—transportation, inventory, movement, waiting, overproduction, over-processing, defects); by reducing variation (using tools such as Six Sigma and Statistical Process Control); by reducing the number of complaints; by standardizing the best way of doing things; or by reducing the cost of poor quality.

- Enter new markets.

- Introduce new products or services.

The above will only work in the medium- and long-term if our product or service is of good quality.

How can a Quality department help an organization earn more money?

The Quality department must show the relationship between quality and financial performance. This can be done in several ways:

- Using the CoQ (cost of quality)/CoPQ (cost of poor quality) framework. This is explained in the next chapter.
- Showing cost saving by preventing complaints, internal non-conformances, and inefficiencies, and by preventing repeat issues.
- Ensuring that the organization gets paid for supplier-related issues. Many organizations recover the material cost of rejected items (by asking for a replacement or requiring suppliers to issue a credit note), but there are often associated costs that are not recovered. These could include the actual disposal cost for scrapped goods, sorting costs, rework costs, or general complaint administration costs. These should be part of a supplier contract in order to ensure there are no arguments when these issues arise.
- Helping an organization's reputation in terms of good quality products or services, and being seen as socially responsible, environmentally friendly, and ethical.

Managers should ask themselves this question. How can we continually improve every aspect of an organization? In answering the question, it is useful to involve the Quality department in supporting, training, and facilitating improvements The Quality department is familiar with developing process flow diagrams, using tools to find the root causes of issues, and ensuring agreed actions are implemented and effective.

We have all heard, and maybe said, that quality is everyone's job. If that is so, where are the quality objectives for engineering, marketing, purchasing, finance, maintenance? How would we determine what these might be? A simple way would be to look at the department concerned and say, "Let us look at the inputs to, and outputs of, your processes. As part of the process of converting inputs to outputs, we will look at how efficiently and effectively the organization's resources are used. Wherever there is waste of a resource, quality is not being achieved." This waste can include things like rework, redesign, replacement POs, excessive call hold time, and delivery delays.

How can we integrate quality into our work? How can each department help achieve the organization objectives above? What does "good quality" look like for each department? Some examples might include:

- In general, all managers should be trained to conduct internal audits and actually perform one or two audits per year. If managers are not comfortable performing an audit, it is acceptable for them to accompany an auditor. This should be part of their individual objectives for the year. If these audits are conducted in their own departments, managers should be at least two levels above the work being reviewed. In many cases, it is better that managers conduct audits in another department (perhaps a department that is a supplier or a customer to their own department). This allows for objectivity and can be a good learning experience for the manager/auditor.

- In general, managers should question the amount of and reason for the work-in-progress material that exists at each step of our processes. Such material can be components or assemblies, but it can also be paperwork.

- In general, managers should question why there are bottlenecks in a process when they walk around. Where are the gates, those items that are holding things back? These should be tackled first if we want to improve our productivity.

- Engineering/Maintenance department—Managers should provide jigs and other capable equipment that is reliable and produces repeatable results in order to ensure that jobs are done correctly and consistently.

- Manufacturing/Production department—Workers should have simple, visual work instructions in order to ensure that all steps in a process or operation are completed correctly before moving to the next step. Each operation should have accurate cycle times and there should be systems in place that ensure we don't only rely on human control.

- Sales/Marketing department—It's essential to have clear customer requirements, including realistic schedules and order dates, and not accept special orders without agreement of the relevant departments.

- Human Resources/Training department—Managers must ensure that employees are adequately trained and should recruit new employees with the right attitude.

- Purchasing department—It's essential to have supplier agreements and explicit requirements on POs; suppliers must demonstrate that their products are of good quality (by means of inspection and test reports or dimensional results).

- Finance/Accounts department—Here quality is determined by cash flow management, minimizing negative exposure to foreign exchange transactions, ensuring the organization gets paid on time and pays on time.

- Quality department—Quality supports all other departments using a "right first time" and "zero defects" mentality.

- Planning department—Here Quality in influenced by inventory turns, WIP values, and quantities.

- Logistics/Stores department—The department influences Quality via correct product location, efficient stock rotation (FIFO), correct identification, and optimization of shipping processes.

By implementing these KPIs, we will ensure that quality is embedded in everyone's work, and this will ensure these activities are aligned to higher level objectives.

Many managers rely on dashboards or trend graphs to review performance. Do the various reports and graphs we receive give us the information we need? Do we know which key metrics we want, and even more importantly, why we want them? Have we explained this to the person or department that is providing this data to us? People should understand why they are required to provide information—they may propose a tweak or a better way of doing something if they understand why. If we don't do this, we may find ourselves asking for reports, and then not using or even viewing them. As senior managers, we should be clear about what we want in terms of KPIs so we don't have to spend time trying to find the information we require or amend the layout of the data. I have worked in organizations where a standard set of monthly data was generated and sent to almost all managers. The people generating the report thought they were doing a great job, although few actually read the data and some just skimmed it. Managers often just look at the traffic lights; if they're green, then that metric is OK and they move on to the next set of data.

A word on data-driven decision making, a phrase that seems to indicate we can either just use quantitative data or let computers make all the decisions. Here is a paraphrase of a quote that captures the inherent weaknesses of this approach; it says that many untalented managers convince themselves that by their mindless application of 'data-driven decision making,' they are good managers. We know that good management is difficult and requires other elements, such as human awareness, good judgement, as well as sound analytical ability. Not everyone has these capabilities. When people claim to be a good manager, but merely managing by the numbers—and exclude the softer factors such as concern for people and creativity—is like claiming to be an artist when painting by numbers.

Another issue to consider is this: How would we rank the following? We might add or remove items (cost efficiency, profit margin, inventory turns), but this list will do for purposes of our discussion.

- Quality
- Health and safety
- On time delivery
- Productivity

This is a false choice. Our goal as senior managers is to integrate these, and our top-level objectives should be ensuring this. For example, why should quality be ranked separately? I believe it should be embedded in productivity. Part of the Quality department's role is to work with the other departments such that:

- It is easier for people to do the job right than wrong
- Production goals are met only when the relevant quality goals are met
- Doing the job correctly minimizes waste in all its forms
- Each department owns its own quality KPIs

The same applies to safety; if quality is not embedded in daily activities, then accidents will inevitably occur.

Measuring anything is just wasted time unless you're prepared to do something useful with the results of that measurement. As the old adage goes:

> *"There should be no inspection without recording,*
> *no recording without analysis, and no analysis without action."*

One problem we have today is that it is so easy to generate data. We have dashboards on our PCs, with sparklines showing trends. We have a multitude of graphs and tables that we either produce or read on a weekly or monthly basis. We can splice information in many ways, and we can mine data, but rarely does anyone take a step back and question why we are collecting this information. There are, of course, times when mining data is useful, but often we should follow the "80/20 rule," separate the vital few from the trivial many, and focus on only the key items.

A related issue has to do with how we present data. We have all seen graphs that baffled us, tables that made no sense, and trends that were based on false assumptions. Even "obvious" information should be questioned. An excellent explanation of how data should be presented can be found in the book by Jon Moon, *Clarity and Impact.* (www.jmoon.co.uk)

Once we have sensibly determined what data we will capture and why, we need to ask ourselves the "so what" question. What will we do with the data and what are the implications of it? It is not enough to collect data and put it into a slideshow at a review meeting, or worse, just file it away. There should be a reason for collecting data in the first place, and this reason should relate to the organization's cascaded objectives. An organization should implement key performance indicators (KPIs) only if it will review them regularly and try to improve the trends. Action must be the result of data that are collected, analyzed, and reviewed. No organization is perfect, operating always at peak performance levels. There is always scope for improvement, and improvement requires action. The next time you are in a review meeting and someone puts up a table or graph or statistic, ask what action is required. If the graph is trending well, maybe no action is required. In these cases ask whether we know what has caused the trend to be good. How do we keep doing it? Is it due to external factors over which we have little control? What are the forces acting on this metric and how might they change in the future?

If the trend is bad, one would expect a discussion to ensue. What factors are behind the trend, and what actions should the organization take to correct them?

Dr. Deming's 14 Points for Management

In his book *Out of the Crisis*, W. Edwards Deming offered 14 key management principles for significantly improving the effectiveness of a business or organization. Many of the principles are philosophical and all are transformative in nature.

These points give plenty of food for thought and discussion, and each could be reviewed as part of a senior management meeting or at sessions specifically held to discuss them.

The 14 Points for Management are condensed here.

1. Create constancy of purpose toward improvement of product and service, with the aim to become competitive, to stay in business, and to provide jobs.

2. Adopt the new philosophy. We are in a new economic age. Western management must awaken to the challenge, must learn its responsibilities, and must take on leadership for change.

3. Cease dependence on inspection to achieve quality. Eliminate the need for inspection on a mass basis by building quality into the product in the first place.

4. End the practice of awarding business on the basis of price tag. Instead, minimize total cost. Move toward a single supplier for any one item, and develop a long-term relationship of loyalty and trust.

5. Improve, constantly and forever, the system of production and service in order to improve quality and productivity and thus constantly decrease costs.

6. Institute on-the-job training.

7. Institute leadership (see Point 12 and Chapter 8). The aim of supervision should be to help people and machines and gadgets to do a better job. Supervision of management is in need of overhaul, as well as supervision of production workers.

8. Drive out fear so that everyone may work effectively for the company (see Chapter 3).

9. Break down barriers between departments. People in research, design, sales, and production must work as a team in order to foresee problems of production and in use that may be encountered with the product or service.

10. Eliminate slogans, exhortations, and targets for the work force asking for zero defects and new levels of productivity. Such exhortations only create adversarial relationships, because most of the causes of low quality and low productivity belong to the system and thus lie beyond the power of the work force.

    • Eliminate work standards (quotas) on the factory floor. Substitute leadership.

    • Eliminate management by objective. Eliminate management by numbers and numerical goals. Substitute leadership.

11. Remove barriers that rob the hourly worker of his right to pride of workmanship. The responsibility of supervisors must be changed from numbers to quality.

12. Remove barriers that rob people in management and in engineering of their right to pride of workmanship. Abolish annual or merit ratings and management by objective (see Chapter 3).

13. Institute a vigorous program of education and self-improvement.

14. Put everybody in the company to work in order to accomplish the transformation. The transformation is everybody's job.

Dr. Deming's 14 Points for Management courtesy of The W. Edwards Deming Institute® (www.deming.org)

CHAPTER SUMMARY

This chapter covered the issue of organization objectives and how quality objectives should cascade from these. We looked at what happens when organizations become inward looking, become focussed on the short term, and have changes in senior management that disrupt the continuity of an organization. We made explicit that the goal of business is to make money, and we proposed that the Quality department support this goal by showing how they can save money for the business, partly by integrating quality into every aspect of an organization's activities. We then looked at how and why we collect data and what we do with it. Finally, we reviewed Deming's 14 points for management.

Questions

1. Do you cascade your mission, vision, and high level objectives to all departments?

2. Are you an inward or outward looking organization?

3. Is there a benefit in doing a SEEQS analysis?

4. What are the quality objectives for every department?

CHAPTER SIX

* * *

Quality Objectives

CHAPTER OUTLINE:

In this chapter we look at some Quality department objectives and discuss why many objectives involve more than one department. We then go on to discuss various ways of measuring trends and results, and the concept of zero defects.

What might be included or excluded from the objectives of the Quality department in your organization?

One key objective of quality should be simplification. Only then can we see the rocks in the water (i.e., the internal and external risks to the organization). There are numerous tools that can be used—tools such as lean, visual control, mistake proofing, simpler layout of documents, common format for documents, fewer documents, simpler organization systems, fewer metrics, supply chain simplification, Kanban, theory of constraints—and they all have merits.

The key to getting best result is to use the most appropriate tool for the situation. Often, these tools are used in isolation, with no overarching thread linking them together. The thread should be the organizational objective of simplifying the systems. When operating in isolation, we achieve the opposite effect—we get people actually adding to the complexity by wanting more resources or by dedicating people specifically to these tasks instead of incorporating the tasks into their daily work routine. We end up with dedicated value stream engineers, when we should be training our existing staff to use the relevant pieces of this philosophy. After all, what is more relevant to a production supervisor than removing waste, in all its forms, from a production process? Why would we bypass them by employing other personnel to perform a key aspect of their role? I am not saying we don't sometimes need the input of an outside expert in particular areas, but our aim should be to instil that knowledge into our own personnel at the appropriate level.

Most organizations and departments have metrics against which they are measured. This is fine when measuring intelligently, when everyone knows what the metrics are, what metrics they are responsible for, and how their role can affect the metrics.

If I am a production manager and one of my metrics is the percentage of product shipped on time, I want to know how many factors can impact that metric. Potential factors include:

- Quality of raw material

- Availability of raw material

- Productivity

- Absenteeism

- Equipment capability, uptime, and capacity

- Clear work instructions

- Trained employees

- The product split required by the customer

- Adequate supporting structures (e.g., no downtime of the organization's computer systems)

How many of these are under my direct responsibility as production manager? I would say, not many of them.

If we want the metrics to apply where appropriate, then we might end up with a metric tree that looks something like that illustrated in Figure 7.

When we reflect on this single metric, we can see that several departments have a part to play if we are to deliver product on time. And we can see that we could drill down further in all cases.

Why are these departments not held to account when one of their functions has caused a product to be shipped late? The answer is often that there is not enough time to drill back through issues; most departments are busy dealing with the next crisis. But it is only by taking the necessary time that we will eliminate or reduce the chances of the same issue recurring. This is where intelligent data collection comes in. We need to know the main issues facing us at any particular time. What are the high-level trends—profitability, cash flow, shipments on time, payments on time? If we have a trend of late shipping, then the review meeting might agree that it should be better understood. The next step is to drill down through our data to see whether the problem is related to domestic or foreign customers, certain customers, certain countries, products with specialized or unique components, or certain departments. Only by doing this will we arrive at accurate information that allows us to implement actions and eliminate the issue.

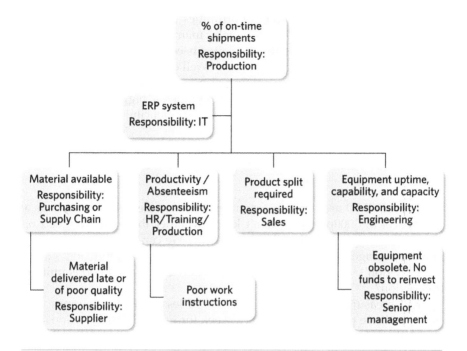

Figure 7   Metric tree for on-time shipments.

I speak about "being held to account." This must be handled as a fact-finding mission, not a blame mission. Nothing will destroy a culture quicker than a "hunt for the guilty" every time something goes wrong. Many people in organizations are doing the best they can, within the restrictions and limitations of their training, budget, manpower, equipment, and management.

A supplier may be sending in poor quality material, but maybe the reason for this is that we supplied vague drawings or specifications or requirements, or perhaps our senior management insisted on using the cheapest supplier. This is another reason why we as managers should not point the finger too quickly; it may end up pointing back at us.

There is another example, mentioned later in the book, of a large organization that had separate departments responsible for manufacturing quality and supplier quality. This resulted in conflicting KPIs. Sometimes things that seem to make sense to senior managers when discussed at the head office do not pan out as intended.

Key Performance Indicators (KPIs) and how we use them

Most KPIs are measured from the organization's point of view instead from that of the customer. KPIs such as percentages, parts per million

(PPM) and defects per million opportunities (DPMO) are not measures of customer satisfaction. Unfortunately, many organizations use these measures. In my experience, they are often used as justification for taking no corrective action. Managers will say, "Well our PPM results are within target so let's move on to something else." Not only is an opportunity missed to correct something before it becomes a bigger issue, but we effectively ignore those customers that are experiencing the problem.

> *Percentage and DPMO KPIs hide a lot of unhappy customers.*

PPM and DPMO are not intuitive measures. If someone says we have a reject level of 3000ppm, we don't know whether that value is good or bad. How many issues does 3000 represent? We can add trend lines and moving average lines, but this often just results in more confusion.

Why don't we keep it simple and measure by finished goods unit, or transaction?

KPI measures should be a factor of 10 less than the volumes. For example, if we produce 1000 units a week (or have 1000 transactions per week), then measuring in percentage is probably OK. If we produce 100 or fewer per week, then using percentages is not OK. Let's look at an example.

Say we produce items that cost $100,000 each and we make about 10 per week. It's not good enough to measure in percentages and say that because we only made one wrong last month our percentage is 97.5 (4 weeks x 10 units = 40 units shipped, with 39 good units). Usually there is a "target" line. How was this target set? Was it someone's opinion or was it based on historical data? If the target is set at 97%, then we could legitimately say that no action is required. Yet we have one customer per month who has received a bad product or service from us and it cost them $100,000. Would you be happy if you spent that amount of money on something and it didn't function as required? Think how annoyed you would be if you received such a product or service and your supplier said, "Well, it's within our target quality level, so we won't be doing anything to fix it." (Sometimes in a situation like this, customer service or Sales personnel will replace or repair the faulty item, possibly at a large cost to the organization. Then, at the management meeting, the Quality or Operations Director will present the graph that shows we're within our Quality target—but not our cost target!)

What happens when we repeat the calculations based on 1000 units per week? If we make one faulty item in a month, now we achieve 99.975% (4 x 1000 = 4000 units shipped, with 3999 good units).

In each of these two examples, we might react differently to the results, based on our expectations, our trends, or our threshold limits.

In both cases, we should be focussing on something else. In both cases, there is one unhappy customer. Instead of saying that "our results for last month are within target, so no action is required," we should be saying, "we have one dissatisfied customer; what action should we take to resolve this and prevent a recurrence?" Of course, the decision might be that no action will be taken, and that might be quite acceptable for the business we are in. My point is that the decision should be arrived at with the customer in mind, and not solely on the internal metrics or the KPIs.

Obviously, the decision about whether action is required depends on the type of product and the industry. One defect might be OK for the dimensions of a desk, but not for a medical device.

Most organizations will set a "target" yield for the year. As we improve, our target might be 99.9% this year, and 99.95% next year. We then find ourselves heading into a situation where we'll be adding more decimal places to targets and showing graphs that start at 98% or 99%. This is one reason why organizations moved to PPM. But moving to PPM is just kicking the can down the road, because it suffers from the same limitations and drawbacks.

Other factors can cloud metrics. Grouping data can be a mistake, especially if it is done at the wrong stage. Let's say we have two sets of data as illustrated in Tables 3 and 4.

In dataset 1, we have issues with production line 1, but we still might consider the results acceptable. Production line 2 might be considered to be performing well.

In dataset 2, we can see that line 2 has significant problems. If we group the data and just show the total percentage, this information is hidden.

The result is tilted towards the first row of data because there are more data points (i.e., we produce more items on line 1). If the largest volume line has the least number of quality problems, the metrics might indicate that all is well, when in fact we could have one or more products on other lines yielding an unacceptable result. The same applies when we produce multiple products on the same lines; the quality of our biggest volume product may mask poor quality on low volume ones.

Table 3 Dataset 1.

	Qty good	Qty bad	Total	Yield (%)
Line 1	562	128	690	81.45%
Line 2	188	16	204	92.16%
Total	750	144	894	83.89%

Table 4 Dataset 2.

	Qty good	Qty bad	Total	Yield (%)
Line 1	562	16	578	97.23%
Line 2	188	128	316	59.49%
Total	750	144	894	83.89%

In fact, intuitively, we might expect this result. If we are making low volumes of a product on an occasional basis, people will be unaccustomed to building it, staff may have changed since it was last built, there may be less supporting tooling and jigs (because it's not economic to build them for low volume orders), and there may be more manual steps in the process. Any of these can increase the risk of errors.

Note: We might even be tempted to average the percentages, but this is mathematically incorrect. If we did this, we would get an answer of 86.80% for table 1 (instead of 83.89%), and 78.36% for table 2, (instead of 83.89%). Data manipulation should be done when the data are in raw form.

Another way of massaging figures is to use percentages rather than actual numbers on graphs. For example, Graph 1 and Graph 2 represent the same set of data illustrated in Table 5, but presented differently.

When a percentage graph is used, the data look "better." This is one reason it might be presented to a customer—or to senior management! But these data are hiding potentially serious problems.

We need to understand that we are choosing one type of data with the aim of presenting ourselves in the best light possible (and there may not be anything inherently wrong in this). My point is this: if we continue to focus on the percentage, we might miss the fact that we are

Table 5   Data table.

	Jan	Feb	Mar	Apr	May	Jun	Jul	Aug	Sep	Oct	Nov	Dec
Qty of defects	13	15	12	18	22	26	28	26	30	32	33	35
Qty produced	200	250	225	320	400	550	600	600	650	750	780	850
% of defects	6.5	6.0	5.3	5.6	5.5	4.7	4.7	4.3	4.6	4.3	4.2	4.1

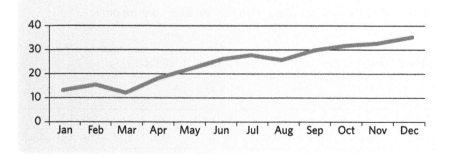

Graph 1   Quantity of defects.

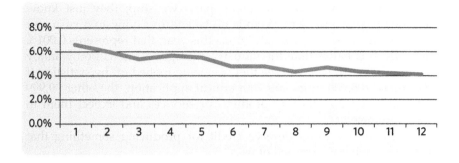

Graph 2 Percentage of defects.

producing excessive defective product every week, and this must be addressed. It is costing us in terms of lost time, remake of parts, possible overtime payments, air freighting product, etc.

It can be argued that it is aspirational to achieve zero defects on a continual basis, but isn't that the role of a target? It's not unachievable on a periodic basis. The graphs could be simple bar charts showing the number of issues or complaints per month. What could be clearer?

There is another issue with PPM, DPMO, and percentage defects. When we use one of these, there is an implication that we should accept a greater number of defects as the volume we make or ship increases (i.e., if we have a target of 1% defects and we make 100 items, then the maximum number of defects allowed is 1; if we make 1000 items, then we are "allowed" 10 defects and still meet our target). But as volume increases, people become more experienced at producing the items or service, they have a greater understanding of the process, and actions have been put in place to prevent repeat non-conformances. It could be argued that the number of non-conformances should be reducing as volume increases. And aren't we building in the wrong attitude by saying that it's OK to have more rejects because we shipped more? If the quality system is good enough, volume should not matter. A robust quality system should produce no repeatable defects, no matter the volume.

If we have implemented a fix but older products still in the market are causing the problem, it can be quite legitimate that we would take no action. We need not issue a recall for every problem that arises, or replace all products in the market with the improved version; in these situations, we must acknowledge that there may be nonconforming products or services problems for some time (even years). But at least we know why the issues are being reported and we can decide how we should respond (give a free replacement, give a new item at a discount, give a refurbished unit free or at a discount).

Customers don't care how many parts we ship; they just know when they have a problem. There is no benefit in saying to a customer "We have already shipped 100,000 units this year; that represents 0.001% defect, which is better than the industry average." This will only annoy customers, because they can see they are being fobbed off by statistics. If one of those 100,000 units fails in a critical application, the other 99,999 don't matter. Customers buy products or services and expect them to work as promised.

Remember, we don't deserve credit for producing something that works; that's what is expected of us.

Sometimes a supplier says, "But you are the only one who has complained or who has this problem." The statement is a classic illustration of an inward-looking organization and it is guaranteed to get the customer's back up. It is almost saying they shouldn't have complained in the first place. Here are three major reasons this is wrong thinking:

1. A customer doesn't care whether anyone else has the same problem; all they care about is that *they* have a problem.

2. How does the supplier know that no one else has the problem? Many consumers do not bother to complain, especially for low cost items; they just never buy from that supplier again.

3. Even if only one customer has this problem, why should that matter in terms of how they are treated?

All of this raises a basic question. Who are our metrics aimed at—the customer, senior management, finance, investors? Although these are all important audiences, we should be looking at it from the customer's point of view. If we do, then we will quickly see that a policy of zero defects is a better approach.

All of the above leads me to believe that more organizations should consider moving toward the zero defects approach (as proposed by Philip Crosby). There are four advantages of using the zero defects approach.

1. It is simple to understand

2. It is not based on the number of units sold

3. It sends the clear message that no complaint or error is acceptable

4. It focuses on the customer, not on the organization's internal measures

In relation to our supporting services (HR, purchasing, logistics, marketing), would we consider our organization to be of good quality if our products or primary services were good but the supporting activities were not? We should not try to cage Quality only into our product or primary service provision. Customers judge us on the whole experience they have with us, from reception or telephone sales to our website, and from Sales and Marketing to after-sales support or servicing. Any of these can break down and cost us lost sales and/or customers. When we look at Quality, we must be holistic in our approach because every department can influence Quality; therefore every department needs quality-related metrics.

A word about system failures, process failures, and people failures

A system is basically a sequence of processes. A basic process (illustrated in Figure 8) has three components. It has at least one input (e.g., energy, material, information, human effort). The transformation step transforms or combines the inputs in some way, resulting in an output—a product (or partial product) or service. The output of one process could be an input to another process—it isn't necessarily a product or service for a customer or end user.

When we look at process failures, we need to look at the quality, reliability, repeatability, and capability of our inputs; then we need to look at the same criteria in relation to the transforming process. If the inputs and transformation process are good, we will expect to have a compliant product or service output.

From a purely process point of view, people can sometimes be a weak link. Our effectiveness is affected by many things:

- We get distracted.
- We get tired.
- We can be in a bad mood.
- We get bored doing repetitive tasks.
- We cannot concentrate for long periods of time.
- We carry bias into our tasks.
- We might not be properly trained.
- We might not think what we do is important and therefore we don't care about our work.
- We know that there is a quality control person at the end of the line to check what we do anyway.

Figure 8   Basic process diagram.

All of this adds up to an organization's most important resource (its people) performing in an imperfect manner simply because of human nature. Our focus needs to be on designing systems to either prevent defects and failure or at least detecting failure before our product or service is delivered to the customer. This is where we look at things such as ergonomics, job enrichment, automation to replace boring and repetitive tasks, job variety, built-in error checks to let people know immediately when something is wrong, and systems designed to prevent a job from being done incorrectly (e.g., a pop-up window to aid in completing an online form). This error-proofing approach is, in my view, a key role for the Quality department.

Cost of (Poor) Quality

Quality KPIs should be converted to cost figures wherever possible. This is the language of business and it is the best way of getting approval for actions that are needed to improve quality or prevent repeat problems. The cost of poor quality (CoPQ) approach is a standard way of doing this.

This approach addresses four costs:

1. Prevention costs—the costs associated with putting systems in place to prevent problems. These can include various aspects of design reviews and validation, supplier quality activities including supplier audits, process validation, Statistical Process Control (SPC), Failure Mode and Effects Analysis (FMEA), operator training, and quality audits.

2. Appraisal costs—the costs associated with inspecting products. These can include incoming inspection, calibration, inspections and tests in production, and product audits.

3. Internal failure costs—the costs found before the product or service has reached the customer. These can include scrap costs, rework, sorting, supplier corrective actions, reject handling and disposition from production, and repair costs.

4. External failure costs (customer complaint costs)—the cost of sorting product at a customer's premises, rework costs, all costs to re-make the product, external certification failures, recall costs, warranty costs, and liability costs.

These are just a few examples of what can be included under each heading. By separating costs into the appropriate category, we can easily show whether quality costs fall on the prevention side or the remediation side. It doesn't mean that we should spend huge sums of money ensuring that, for example, suppliers never send us reject material (to ensure this, we might have to install our own personnel at the supplier's premises or insist that every product is tested 100%, for which the supplier would charge us). But I think it's reasonable to say that for many organizations, quality costs fall more on the appraisal and failure side than on the prevention side. As we go from (a) to (d) in the list above, costs usually increase, so it makes sense to focus more on prevention and appraisal costs.

Associated with this is the concept of dividing KPIs into leading and lagging indicators. Leading indicators can include things such as internal audits, calibration, preventive maintenance, or process capability studies. Lagging indicators (those that happen after the event) include the number of internal rejects or number of complaints. Leading indicator items tend to be associated with prevention costs. It makes sense to invest more in preventive measures because with these systems in place, we will avoid having to scrap, rework, or repeat any process. In our own organizations, how many leading and lagging indicators do we have in place? Could we move some of the lagging ones to leading ones? What would be the cost benefit in doing that?

When looking at metrics for the Quality department, we should not look at the number of complaints, the number of product non-conformances, or the number of audit non-conformances. Why? Because most customer complaints are not caused by the Quality department. These issues are organization failures that involve one or more other departments. This is where many organizations go wrong and never see continual improvement, because these issues are allocated to Quality, as was discussed earlier. We could possibly make the number of repeat issues a Quality department metric, because the Quality department might be responsible for ensuring that the corrective actions are robust enough to prevent repeat issues.

So what might we consider metrics for the Quality department? One thing we could look at is how the Quality department imparts knowledge into the organization so that everyone can take responsibility for quality. Transfer of ownership is key. This has tended to happen more with areas such as health and safety (and even environment) than with quality. For too long, we have believed that we must have a dedicated department to handle all quality-related issues. There are good reasons for having a Quality department (discussed in more detail in Chapter 8) but it's equally important to move some issues out of Quality and into the relevant area or department. For example, why don't we train people how to write procedures, and then let them draw up their own procedures or work instructions? There is still a role for the Quality department in terms of making sure client, regulatory, and quality management system (QMS) criteria are met, but we should look at it being more of a review role rather than that of originator.

Another, and perhaps more obvious role for the Quality department has to do with root cause analysis and problem solving. The Quality department has tools that can be used to help with these issues, but it should be training up other departments so that they can perform these analyses themselves.

Other examples are mistake-proofing and visual control techniques. It has been argued that Quality departments should be quite small and focus on those things that they are best placed to do. For other things, such as those listed above, we should consider transferring them to the relevant departments.

One issue that is very culture-dependent is that of inspection. Traditionally, this role has been part of Quality Control, but having the Production department take responsibility is a sign of advanced organizational culture. This requires a major shift in thinking—we need to consider how to build in more mistake-proofing and more auto-detection of errors, and explain to inspectors and other employees that finding mistakes is a good thing; not only does it stop a bad product or service from reaching the external customer, but it also allows us to put in an action to prevent recurrence. It would also result in saving on indirect labor. Remember that no amount of inspection will make the product or service any better. The only way to improve quality is to improve the process.

> *It has been said that the level of inspection in an organization is an indication of the level of trust you have in your processes.*

We should be reviewing all our support departments and asking whether they need to be so large. Why? In *Building the Invisible Quality Corporation*, Kevin R. Maromonte argues that after re-assigning the traditional roles performed by a Quality department, the remaining activities in the Quality department could be handled by just one person, a VP of Quality.

Improved quality levels will result in cost savings due to reduced rework, reduced numbers of defects, reduced volume of complaints, reduced WIP and inventory levels, reduced cycle time, reduced inspection costs, reduced total costs, and reduced calibration costs. These are metrics that can be measured and tracked.

Assuming we agree that all areas of an organization need to perform with a quality mentality, we must ask ourselves this question. What quality metrics exist in each department? For example, what might be the quality metrics for a customer service department? Quality requires more than just answering queries within x minutes or performing short term corrective actions within y hours and long-term corrective action within *z* hours. What about the quality of response? Is it professional? Does it give customers the information they need? Is the long-term corrective action implemented and effective (i.e., does it prevent recurrence)? Do we follow up with the customer to make sure issues have been addressed satisfactorily? Is it easy for customers to contact us? Are they able to contact us 24/7, if necessary? Do we provide online forms and online chat facilities?

If we want to embed quality into every department, then each department and process should have one or more quality-related KPIs.

Appendix 3 includes a list of traditional KPIs. Many of them don't actually belong to Quality, even though they are often thought to.

Senior management should look at an organization's objectives to determine whether they:

- Are still relevant

- Are attributed to the right department(s)

- Contribute to the aims of the organization

- Avoid conflicting with objectives lower down the organization chain and triggering the law of unintended consequences

Let's look at some typical customer non-conformances that occur in a manufacturing organization. How many are caused by the Quality department?

- Damaged parts

- Faulty parts

- Wrong quantity

- Wrong color

- Wrong spec part delivered

- Wrong part number delivered

- Incorrect paperwork—invoice, packing slips, customs documentation

- Incorrect packaging

- Missing parts/incomplete order

- Incorrect price

Let's look at it another way. If an invoice is wrong, do we take the issue away from the finance/accounting department and hand it over to the Quality department to sort out? Generally we don't, so why do we do it with manufacturing issues? If the root cause department is not QA, then why do we ask QA to sort it out? Why do we not ask the relevant department to handle the problem—both short term (containment) and long term (prevention of recurrence)? By handing it off, we reinforce the idea of Quality as police officers, as a department people only see when something is wrong. And we allow those responsible to avoid the issue.

What we should say to the relevant department is this: "You are responsible for this non-conformance; therefore, this issue is being added to your KPI. Any repeat of this issue will result in your department score (and possibly the department manager's bonus) being affected." There may be a role for Quality in that the responsible department might ask QA to help with the investigation or the root cause analysis or the preparation of a report back to the customer. But the Quality department is no longer seen as responsible for resolving these issues.

Having proposed this approach, I see two issues that must be considered before implementing it.

We must avoid creating a blame culture and instead develop a four-part process: identify the responsible department; encourage people from within and outside that department to suggest improvement actions; let the responsible department request help from Quality (or any other department) if appropriate; and investigate and establish the root cause. Then the responsible department can present the corrective action. Implementation of corrective action will often involve other departments and should include both a start date and a review date to verify that the implemented action has been effective.

Another issue to beware of is that people might try to pass a quality problem on to another department so it doesn't affect their own KPIs. This represents an inherent immaturity on the part of department managers and it is up to senior management to resolve this. Do senior managers want departmental managers to act as if they have been given a hot coal to carry, and watch them try and pass it on to someone else? Or do they want their departmental managers reaching out to grab any issues that come up? If we want the latter, then we must reward the latter; up to now, we have often rewarded the former. Why don't we reward managers or departments for every issue for which they take ownership? If done right, this could create a virtuous circle, with people actively trying to take on issues.

To recap, the objectives of the Quality department should be some combination of the following:

- To help transfer ownership of quality to all departments
- To assist in setting quality objectives for every department and manager
- To help reduce waste and variation
- To help make processes more robust
- To support the organization's aim for zero defects

- To simplify operations
- To streamline documentation
- To be an internal consultant for other departments
- To train people in root cause analysis, continual improvement, risk analysis, and problem solving
- To ensure all regulatory and compliance issues are met
- To be the voice of the customer (VOC) and keep the organization customer-focussed
- To promote the concept of the internal customer
- To set and review metrics that have an internal and external customer focus
- To demonstrate the link between poor quality and poor organization performance
- To help departments devize and implement long term corrective actions
- To develop visual control systems and prevention strategies
- To make it easier to do a job right than wrong
- To encourage people to ask why things are done in a certain way, and not be afraid to question the status quo
- To develop suppliers
- To help embed a quality attitude across the organization
- To encourage design for manufacture, design for assembly, design for Test
- To show people how to have visual controls and mistake proofing

CHAPTER SUMMARY

In this chapter we reviewed some of the key objectives for the Quality department, and we showed that many Quality objectives require the input of more than one department. As senior managers, we need to be aware of this, and set the objectives so as not to give conflicting messages. We looked at the disadvantages of using DPMO and PPM and percentage as measures, before moving on to discuss people and process failures. We then looked at having quality objectives built into the objectives of every department, before discussing a new approach to making departments responsible for issues. Finally, we looked at potential objectives for a QA department.

Questions

1. Does your organization have outward-looking KPIs?

2. Would you consider your organization to be of good quality if your products and services were good but the supporting activities were not (e.g., HR, purchasing, logistics, marketing)?

3. Do quality objectives cascade from the organization's objectives?

4. Do you have a culture where people try to avoid or ignore issues?

CHAPTER SEVEN

* * *

The Role of Departments

CHAPTER OUTLINE:

In this chapter, we look at why we have departments, we discuss the silo mentality that exists in many organizations, and we look at the conflicting KPIs that are often the result of efforts by well-intentioned senior management. We also illustrate Greiner's growth model for organizations.

Departments can be hotbeds of resistance, friction, and suboptimization. Should we get rid of departments entirely? Or is the problem KPIs that are neither aligned to the organization as a whole nor aligned with those of other departments? For example, do we tell the purchasing department that although quality and on-time delivery (OTD) are important, the key thing they will be measured on (and rewarded for) is price and cost savings? What is the obvious result of such a situation? The result will be that Quality will find it hard to get the Purchasing department to lean on suppliers when there are quality issues, especially if one of the Purchasing department's metrics is the number of supplier issues. This last item creates a conflict for the Purchasing department. If they are measured on the number of quality issues, there is an inherent drive to minimize issues brought to them by the Quality department. The result is an internal battle within the organization, between two departments trying to prove that the issue is or is not due to the supplier. This is not good planning by senior management. Yet these types of situations are created by well-intentioned and intelligent people who thought they were doing the right thing. It might be the right thing, when considered in isolation, but a department's KPIs must be set and viewed in relation to other departments or there will be problems. Organizations need to wake up to these contradictory KPIs if they want to archive superior corporate performance.

There is often no holistic approach to the metrics we use, and the result is suboptimization.

I worked for a large organization with exactly this problem. The internal quality function was independent of the supplier quality function. When problems arose, there was a battle for each side to prove its case. The supplier Quality department were measured on the number of supplier issues, so it was in their interest to keep this number as low as possible. The operator on the line said items arrived with quality problems, so the internal quality person insisted the problem was a supplier issue. The supplier quality guy didn't believe this, suggesting the operator had the damaged items or that the damage was caused in the warehouse when unloading or storing or issuing the component.

It can be hard to definitively prove one of these possible scenarios, so we end up with either a big delay in getting back to a supplier, or we waste time talking to everyone involved, or the component is scrapped, with no further investigation.

If we want to overcome this situation, we have two options:

1. *We set up an agreed method of investigation, outlining how issues are to be investigated and what evidence is to be collected, or*

2. *We bring the supplier Quality department under the Quality department.*

Where departments exist, there are silos. We need to balance this against the expertise that comes with specialization. This is a key decision area for senior management—to define that line and to subsequently determine whether we achieve the cost savings and efficiencies that were envisaged. For example, if a problem is found and the solution might require a design modification, what investigation, actions, and proof are required before such an issue can be handed to and accepted by the R&D department? Is R&D obliged to take action? How quickly do they need to address the issue; how is it prioritized? Is there visibility on when and how the issue is addressed?

On a more general note, how do we determine whether we have conflicting KPIs in our own organizations? Are there any such conflicts within our own department?

Most departments are reluctant to take on issues and tend to throw up roadblocks, often raising seemingly valid questions. How many issues have been found, how many have been found by the customer, what's the percentage of failures based on the quantity shipped (an old favorite argument that is regularly used), has someone checked the bill of materials, how is the part handled, are the work instructions sufficient, etc. One or more of these can indeed be valid questions, but they are asked with an inward-looking intent. How can I kick this away and stop it getting into my department and thus becoming an issue that I have to deal with? How can I stop this affecting my department's KPI or my bonus? Metric-driven management systems have fostered this attitude and it is only by our actions that this can be changed.

Senior management need to resolve this early on, because once such attitudes take hold, it will be very hard to change them. We may have to actively reward situations where departments take on unexpected issues, and this attitude must be built into the department KPI. Departments often look for absolute proof of a problem and collect a ton of data before even looking at an issue. Sometimes this is valid, but we need to look at the intent of posing these questions. Sometimes the right approach is to take immediate action (maybe because one or two major customers have complained), rather than bog down the process by looking for extensive test and field data. The opportunity to act might be very short, and if we want to keep those customers, we need to do something now, not in six month's time. This can be hard for technical departments, which tend to focus excessively on data while ignoring the market or commercial impacts of delaying action. It is the job of senior management to decide what is best for the organization, even if that means overriding the data collection stage or accepting responsibility for the issue. Common sense and commercial sense must prevail.

It has been argued that cross functional teams work better for customers than functional departments. If this is so, why should we keep functional departments? Should we consider more cross functional departments throughout the organization, focussing on key customers, regions, markets, and product lines? This thinking has led to matrix organization structures, where Quality, Operations, Purchasing, and Finance are in a single office. This can be done based on customer or geographical region, or product line, or industry served, etc., and is often very effective in terms of inter-departmental communication. In my own experience, there is a lot to be gained by having appropriate departments in the same space. Removing the physical barrier between departments fosters better communication. Having departments in the next building or on another floor is sufficient to create a communication block and departments end up communicating by email. Email should never be a substitute for face-to-face discussion.

Of course, some departments must stand alone and others can be shared; supporting departments such as IT, Purchasing, and HR are obvious examples of shared services. This is how many large organizations work, because it allows centralisation and the head office structure. There may be nothing wrong with this set up, but we need to be conscious of why we have the structure we have. We should ask whether it is it still relevant and know, as we go down the organization tree, at what level we need to break out of this centralized structure. Do the support departments effectively support the other departments? We can all think of circumstances where this support didn't exist or was insufficient or too slow or too bureaucratic.

There are various models of how structure changes as an organization grows and the challenges it faces at key moments. One of these is Larry E. Greiner's "six phases of growth" model (Figure 9).

Phase 1: Growth through Creativity

This is where the organization is small, with informal reporting structures. Eventually, as the organization grows, there can be a leadership crisis, where professional management is required. Often, someone new is brought in to tackle this.

Phase 2: Growth through Direction

As growth continues, more formal structures such as budgets, marketing, and production are introduced. Eventually, with numerous products and/or processes, one person cannot manage everything and this results in an autonomy crisis. New structures, with delegation, are required.

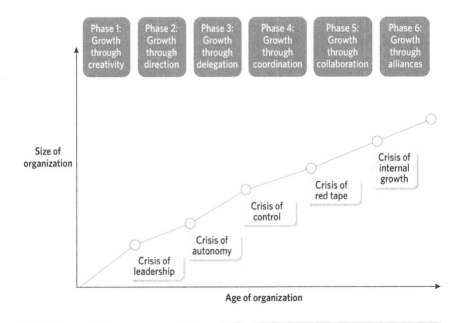

Figure 9 Greiner's model of organizational growth.

Phase 3: Growth through Delegation

The original owners/managers can find it hard to fully let go, and the resulting control crisis is often solved by coordination.

Phase 4: Growth through Coordination

Here we see things like central services and support structures. This stage can result in a red tape crisis. The culture and structure need to be reviewed.

Phase 5: Growth through Collaboration

This could be reflected in things like a matrix structure with information systems and team-based financial rewards. This phase ends with a crisis of internal growth.

Phase 6: Growth through Alliances

Growth may continue through merger, outsourcing, networks, and other solutions involving other companies.

Growth rates will vary between and even within phases. The duration of each phase depends almost totally on the rate of growth of the market in which the organization operates. The longer a phase lasts, though, the harder it will be to implement a transition.

Often, when an organization grows to a large size, it will split up into separate business units that operate like separate organizations, and thus the Greiner cycle gets repeated.

As an overarching approach, departmental managers should:

- Own their processes, including what happens when things go wrong, either internally or with a customer.
- Own the implementation of any corrective or preventive actions.
- Own the performance metrics for their department.
- Own the knowledge found in every department, knowledge that is gained by experience and often not written down anywhere. Department managers must be aware of this and consider how to pass knowledge on as people leave or retire. One option is to ask people to prepare documents or presentations or short training courses on their areas of expertise. This can help spread the knowledge while giving the expert an opportunity for recognition

(and possible small rewards). This can be effective when knowledge owners who have been with the organization for some time near retirement. Many organizations support continuing education for subject matter experts (SMEs) to ensure that their knowledge remains current in the field. These SMEs should take the initiative to identify educational opportunities for themselves, and take responsibility for passing on their knowledge to others in the department. When organizations cut back on the training budget, they should "red circle" the process owners to ensure that they are exempt from the budget cut.

There should be at least one back-up SME for each department. We should never rely on just one person for knowledge that is critical for the organization. For large organizations, it's important to know how knowledge is built up, retained, documented, and disseminated.

CHAPTER SUMMARY

Here, we looked at how KPIs can often result in sub optimisation of an organization's performance, can cause inter-departmental conflict, and can generate unintended consequences. We also looked at Greiner's organizational growth model.

Questions

1. Does your organization or department have conflicting KPIs? How do you know? Where is the evidence?

2. Have you considered the merits of a matrix structure?

3. Do your support departments effectively support other departments, or is everything too centralized even at the user level?

4. If you say that quality is everyone's responsibility, does this mean you should get rid of the quality department and every department KPIs that reflect a quality product or service? Or would there still be a role for the quality department?

CHAPTER EIGHT

✳ ✳ ✳

The Role of the Quality Department

Before we even question the role of the Quality department, let us ask ourselves this question. Why do we have or need a Quality department? Asking this fundamental question can result in interesting points of view and can become an almost philosophical debate on Quality. This is healthy. The aim of the discussion is not to require people to justify their existence but to simply improve how we do things. That is the starting point. It could end up with a reduced or enlarged size or role for the Quality department. This same fundamental question can be asked of all supporting departments (IT, HR, Training, Legal, Planning).

Answering this question might result in the organization taking a number of actions:

- Leaving things as they are;

- Getting rid of the Quality department altogether;

- Increasing the size or role of the Quality department;

- Decreasing the size or role of the Quality department; or

- Outsourcing the Quality function.

Before eliminating the Quality function, we need to think about the tasks currently done by that function. How will these be absorbed into the rest of the organization? Certain tasks cannot be avoided if we are ISO 9001 certified or in a regulated industry. We have all heard the cliché that "Quality is everyone's responsibility," but there is a massive gap between using this phrase and putting a coherent and effective structure in place to implement it.

If we decide to outsource the Quality function, how might we do this? We could ask the current Quality team to set up as contractors or we might employ a Quality consultant or Quality inspectors/auditors.

If we agree on the need for a Quality department, we should determine what its responsibility is and, equally important, what its responsibility *is not.*

There is no debate over whether departmental managers should be responsible for departmental budgets, for health and safety in their department, for the right number and calibre of people, or for the right selection of computers and other equipment. Why should quality be any different?

If the Quality department is seen as a value-adding department, we should look for benefits such as these:

- The organization now has a consistent way of doing things, thus reducing errors.

- Employees are encouraged to question why things are done in a certain way and why certain documents are needed, and to suggest how things could be improved.

- All departments understand proper corrective action—root cause analysis and problem solving techniques.

- All departments understand proper preventive action—feeding into Failure Modes and Effects Analysis (FMEA) and control plans, Standard Operating Procedures (SOP), calibration—and thus reduced failure costs.

- Well-developed suppliers supply high quality products.

- The organization benefits from improved equipment capabilities and system robustness.

- A quality attitude is embedded throughout the organization (this can only be done by visible support from all the senior management).

- Departments enjoy an increased use of visual control and mistake proofing.

- The organization has enhanced customer focus.

- Departments make use of techniques such as design for manufacture, design for assembly, design for use.

- The organization uses internal audits to look at how to reduce costs and improve processes.

The Quality department should be pushing ideas such as simplifying procedures and processes, visual control systems, risk reduction, and reducing variation. The Quality department might still do things like document control and calibration, but these could be moved to other departments. Nothing is so sacred that it cannot be changed if there is a benefit in doing so.

Quality should be a support function, providing useful information, being a resource, carrying out training, being the internal voice of the customer (VOC), and translating customer or regulatory requirements into meaningful requirements for each department.

Quality issues very often arrive via the Quality department, whether they be customer complaints or rejects detected by quality inspectors or auditors. This makes people think that the issues belong to QA, and it can be very hard to move them to the department that is actually responsible. If customers knew the names of people in the key departments, would we let them contact those people directly? Many organizations are afraid of how these departments might communicate with customers. Some might try to blame the customer or admit liability, or try to minimize the impact, or reveal too much information. Maybe the response might not be robust enough to prevent recurrence, or the department might not communicate or document the issue or the actions. These are all management issues; we can train key people in each department in how they should respond to customer issues.

When we think of ourselves as customers, would we not be delighted to talk to the relevant manager when we have a problem? For example, if we buy components from a supplier and they are delivered too late, would we not rather talk to the supplier's logistics department than to their Quality department? The Quality department can only look into it and get back to us; the logistics department could tell us the reason for the delay and when we can expect delivery. See how this shortens the communications route and the route to resolution?

Having a Quality department seems to foster a mentality of "the Quality department is responsible for quality issues." This has been addressed earlier, but let me just repeat. Because quality as a concept is so broad, it's difficult to determine where responsibility should lie.

Department managers know they are responsible for running their budget, for ensuring staff work in a safe manner and have adequate training. But how often do we see aspects of quality written into their job specs? This, for me, is a key reason why quality issues do not get addressed as well as they might, and why people in the Quality department continually complain that it is they who have to drive meetings and actions relating to quality issues. We might rely on our Quality department to be the gatekeeper and to be the key department protecting our organization from unnecessary risks, but they cannot do this alone. And if QA *are* to perform this task, it's important to anticipate some of the negative consequences:

- They are perceived as the police and thus "not on the same team" as Operations.

- They become excessively conservative in order to ensure they don't let anything out that might expose the department or the organization.

- Relying on a department means we're relying on people, and people are not always 100% effective; non-conformances will still reach customers. Process-based solutions are needed.

These are not desirable outcomes, and I would contend that a fundamental change is needed in the role of QA in order to overcome these issues. Let us look at how we might start to address this.

One way of moving forward might be to change the name of the Quality department to something else:

- Quality resource department

- Quality improvement department

- Performance improvement department

- Business systems department

- Continual improvement department

- Organization improvement department

- Business improvement department

By using one of these names, we might better focus on what the Quality department is, and is not, responsible for. Just as important, it changes how people think of the Quality department. It moves attitudes toward an improvement philosophy, positions Quality as a resource department, and allows Quality to overarch all activities of an organization.

   Each department should be responsible for its own procedures, forms, flow charts, and so on. It makes little sense to have these documents drawn up by another department. Quality can help by ensuring the documents are clear, simple, effective, robust, auditable, and consistent across all departments and that they meet any statutory or regulatory requirements. The Quality department can also focus on training, document control, and knowledge sharing (promoting tools and techniques that help people find root causes or prevent repeat instances). But Quality should not develop procedures in isolation; it should propose a document structure or layout and then help other departments draw up their own documents within that framework.

I also propose a re-evaluation of the Quality department's traditional roles and suggest that there are many other areas where Quality personnel can support the organization. QA personnel have skills that are readily transferable to other departments and work areas, and we should be setting up structures to allow them to work with other departments. If we want to get more benefit from our Quality department, why not use quality personnel as internal continual improvement consultants and advocates? Doesn't every department want to improve? If the answer to this is "yes," then why not consider transferring a quality person into another department for a few weeks or months? Bring them in and say, "We want to improve how we do things in this department, we want to reduce waste and variation, we want to streamline our processes and cut down on paperwork, we want to resolve issues that have been repeating, and we want to introduce a culture of continual improvement." Is this not part and parcel of what Quality personnel do as their day job? This helps instil the philosophy of quality as a value-adding activity.

Quality personnel also need to show how they contribute to the bottom line. This is not always easy to do, but attempts should be made to show the costs and cost savings associated with quality issues. Cost savings and cost avoidance are often used to justify Six Sigma projects, so it's just a matter of applying the same financial techniques to other issues. Quality personnel tend to show only the results of their work in trend graphs and Pareto charts, but senior management should ensure the finance managers work closely with QA to translate the metrics into financial values and financial impacts. Quality personnel should publicize their successes and not wait to be called to account for or justify their existence. It should be clear to the whole organization how quality is helping overall performance.

The Quality department is not responsible for actions outside of its control. For example, the Quality department is not responsible if people do not follow procedures and instructions, if operators are moved to a different area and not retrained, if the supporting system is inadequate (poor lighting, poor information sharing), if there is a blame culture, if there is no teamwork, if people only want to maximize their own department's performance no matter what, if managers or leaders won't listen, if there is no re-investment in equipment, if the tools are inadequate, if unsuitable people are hired, and if customer complaints are ignored.

Although each of these issues might impact on quality, they belong to a different department; in the final analysis, they are the responsibility of senior management.

Any one or combination of these factors could be the root cause behind a product recall or a batch of material that has to be scrapped. The challenge is to create a system that allows us to quickly drill down to the root cause, and this is where tools such as "5 whys" can be very useful.

Quality managers have traditionally been poor at building the business case for quality—linking quality objectives to organization objectives. This might be because many quality managers were engineers previously and feel safer in the world of data and data manipulation. Any engineer moving into a managerial position should be coached in the financial and people aspects of management. As an aside, why don't we ask each department to prepare presentations on what they do, how they contribute to the organization, and how they can help other departments? For example, it would be really useful if the finance department were to run short courses on the basics of financial accounts, and to give examples of how to show the cost benefits or cost avoidance of each department's activities.

The Quality department needs to demonstrate value, in money terms. What is the ROI in terms of quality? How can the Quality department contribute to profit? Are these questions ever asked in your organization?

As was discussed in the "What is quality?" chapter, there is often confusion over what constitutes a quality issue. Some people say late deliveries, incorrect documentation, transport damage, and bad packaging are examples of bad quality. The phrase "poor quality" can be applied to anything that is wrong. Many organizations rely on the Quality department to coordinate these types of investigations and agree on corrective actions. But these investigations should be led by the responsible department, with Quality personnel supporting and involved in the investigation, ensuring effective actions are agreed to and implemented, and giving an independent and expert review of the conclusions.

The goal should be for the Quality department to focus on continual improvement across all departments, and generate a Business Management System (BMS) or Organization Management System (OMS). In this way, Quality can help the business to implement its strategy.

There is a lot to be gained when the Quality department conducts fewer audits and other department managers do more. I suggest that more senior managers accompany the Quality person during an audit. It would be an eye-opening experience. Managers would see that the systems we set up often frustrate users or prevent them from providing the optimum customer service. Layered process audits (where various levels of management conduct audits) can be a good approach to this. These types of audits provide several benefits:

- Managers conducting the audit develop an appreciation of what is involved in certain tasks and processes.

- People being audited have a chance to show how good they are at their work, and to make suggestions directly to a manager.

- The manager has an opportunity to ask questions that would not be asked by the quality auditor—why certain tasks are done, or done in a particular way, or how that process helps achieve department or organizational objectives.

These types of audits, though often quite effective, must be planned. Auditees need to know who will be involved. They should be people who do not feel threatened when a manager or director is part of the audit team. For their part, auditors must not focus on finding things wrong with another department, and they must not audit the person. They must remember that they are auditing the system, a system that is the responsibility of management. They are there to observe and ask questions, knowing that improvement suggestions and actions will arise from the audit.

A few words about inspection

Let me start with that well-known phrase: "Why is there never enough time to do a job properly the first time around, but there is always enough time to do it again?"

Inspecting products has traditionally been the remit of the Quality department; in some organizations, production people carry out the first inspection and this is followed by a Quality inspection. Organizations could save time and money by ensuring that the production inspection is as thorough as that carried out by quality inspectors. The traditional argument against this is that people shouldn't inspect their own work. (The unspoken reason is, "you can't trust the operators.")

There is an easy way around the first part of this argument. For example, in a situation with three processes (A, B, and C, each with its own operator), one solution would be to define the key quality aspects of each process and then ask the operator at B to inspect output from process A, the operator at C to inspect output from process B, and so on. This can be done for all processes, leaving only the final process output to be checked. From a quality point of view, we should design systems and processes that prevent incorrect items or service from passing to the next process; if something non-conforming is produced, it is detected at that station.

Not trusting operators is a management and culture issue, and should be dealt with separately at management level.

Taking a step back from this, have we ever asked ourselves why we inspect? It seems to me that there are two reasons for inspection:

1. We do not have confidence in our people, and/or

2. We do not have confidence in our process.

How might we approach these issues? Let us work on the basis that people do not deliberately want to do a bad job. With this starting point, we can see that it is the responsibility of management to provide the training, resources, and infrastructure to ensure that people can do the job properly. We should not be blaming the employee. As for lack of confidence in our process? If this is the problem, then it is clearly down to management to resolve it.

We need to ensure our equipment and processes are statistically capable (by conducting capability studies), and then monitor the situation via tools such as Statistical Process Control (SPC). It's also important to practice preventive maintenance and to look for opportunities for improvement. A lot can be done through the Engineering and Quality departments to use more visual controls and to mistake-proof and make processes more robust.

Some organizations also have a customer service department. Is this department necessary? Does the name not suggest that other departments are not doing what they should? Other departments and functions in an organization already deal with customers directly, so why can these not handle customer issues? Often, a customer service department will pass on an issue to another department anyway, resulting in a communication triangle instead of a straight line. More time and money wasted.

Then we end up with the customer service scenarios illustrated in Figures 10 and 11.

What about considering the improved scenario illustrated in Figure 12?

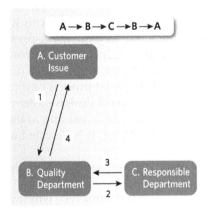

Figure 10 Traditional communications triangle.

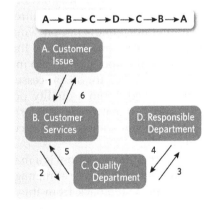

Figure 11 Traditional communications triangle with extra link.

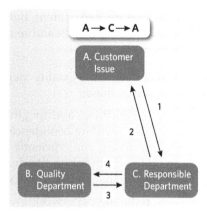

Figure 12 New communications triangle—consultation with B or informing B.

The Quality department is responsible for establishing and measuring the effectiveness of the ISO 9001 quality management system via ongoing metrics, internal audits, and the management review. But we need to be clear about the value of this review. What do we want to get out of it, information or plans for action? If it's only for information, then we need to question the benefit of having the certification. We need improvement actions to result, not just nice graphs or tables.

One of the key failings of a Quality department can be lack of communication with others. They sometimes hoard info, sometimes don't analyze it fully (don't take the information to its logical conclusion), sometimes just email it out or present the high level stuff, or sometimes just beaver away in their own silo without involving others. They don't meet with the relevant managers, the ones who have the power and responsibility to do something about it. Ultimately, this is a structural and cultural issue within an organization. If the behaviors and actions are not what we would like, there is usually a reason behind them; that reason is often either lost in the past or can be directly attributable to certain individuals. As senior managers, we need to find out which is the case and take appropriate action to eliminate sub-standard communication.

Should the Quality department be seen as a cost or as a value-added department?

There are obviously costs related to having a Quality department. Usually the biggest cost is wages, but there can be other large costs such as inspection, measuring, or test equipment (covered under capex); special software; calibration costs; or specific training requirements. It used to be the case that the cost of poor quality (scrap, sort, rework costs) was attributed to the Quality department, but most organizations have moved on from this incorrect approach and re-allocated the costs to where the issues were generated.

Quality as value adding is where the Quality department should be focusing, looking at issues such as these:

- Performing value added auditing, auditing that helps those being audited as well as providing confidence that processes are operating correctly, effectively, and efficiently (not just auditing because there is an audit schedule); audits should be a core part of an organization's risk management strategy.

- Simplifying systems, reducing paperwork.

- Creating visual controls.

- Supporting other departments in effective root cause analysis allowing for long term corrective action and preventive action.

- Helping other departments to be more self-sufficient from a process and product quality point of view. This means training other departments to draw up their own flow charts, procedures and forms; deal with customer complaints; carry out internal audits; and find the root causes of rejected items.

- Supporting other departments so that customer, regulatory, or certification criteria are met.

- Being proactive in reducing risk and variation.

The next bit is to determine how to convert these activities into financial terms—for both cost savings and cost avoidance. To do this, we need to measure baseline data first.

For example, if we want to introduce more visual control of stock, we should first determine the extent of the problem:

1. What quantity of stock ends up being scrapped because it has expired or has been superseded by a later revision?

2. How much time is spent looking for parts that are not where they should be?

3. How much time is lost looking for parts that are mislabelled?

4. How often do we fail to follow FIFO (first in, first out) inventory guidelines? This may not seem like a problem, but consider the example of parts that come in either on a reel or in boxes of say, 100. We issue out a full box or reel. It is often the case that the full quantity is not used, so the unused parts are returned to the stores. For organizations that ignore FIFO, the easy option

next time is to issue out a full reel or box rather than the partial quantity plus a full reel or box. After a while, even though the stock count might be accurate, it might consist of a multitude of partial reels or boxes. Eventually, this creates long setup delays on the line, where many partial reels must be used in order to complete a job. There are also traceability issues caused by having so many reels or boxes with different lot numbers.

If senior management decide to change the role of QA, the Quality department personnel should be reassured that the changes are changes in role only and will not result in layoffs. For many organizations, there may be very little, if any, change in role or day-to-day activities. Some of these "new" activities are:

- Training employees in problem solving, internal auditing, root cause analysis, basic SPC, mistake proofing, and visual controls.

- Moving from being seen as "the police" to being seen as helpers, as people who can contribute to the more effective and efficient running of any department or process. Becoming the first people to call when help is required.

- Maintaining, simplifying, and streamlining the QMS—not just running it.

- Getting more involved in risk management and prevention strategies for the organization.

- Looking at integrating various management systems (Quality, Environmental, Health and Safety, Information Security, etc.).

- Continuing to ensure that all regulatory and customer requirements are met, and providing calibration and document and record control.

- Transferring ownership of Quality issues (complaints) to the relevant departments, with the Quality department acting as a resource and internal consultant.

- Working with departments to build up robustness (i.e., ensuring that there is more than one gate to prevent problems getting out, or that problems are prevented or detected at source).

Senior managers who consider the Quality department a cost and believe they need that department only because of certification or customer requirements are missing the whole point. There is a huge benefit to be had from a well-trained and experienced Quality department—it's just a question of aligning them and setting goals.

> *To get the best from your Quality department, train them well and then let them loose in your organization, saying, "Your job is to improve all aspects of how we operate. You will be measured by the costs avoided or saved, by reducing paperwork and bureaucracy, and by transferring ownership of quality to every department."*

CHAPTER SUMMARY

In this chapter we looked at the roles, responsibilities, and limitations of the responsibilities of the Quality department. We considered new roles, and we emphasized that the Quality department needs to demonstrate a contribution to the organization. We looked at the quality communications triangle, we discussed whether the Quality department should be considered an overhead or a value-add function, and we considered using other names for the department, to show its broader remit and contribution.

Questions

1. Why does your organization have (or not have) a Quality department?

2. How do you get more benefit from your Quality department?

3. Should the Quality department have a new name?

4. How does your Quality department save costs or avoid costs?

5. Have you, as senior managers, ever accompanied a person from the Quality department during an audit? If not, why not?

CHAPTER NINE

* * *

Quality and Its Relationship with Other Departments

CHAPTER OUTLINE:

In this chapter we look at how we can start to embed quality into various departments, so that everyone is operating in a "quality" way. The areas of purchasing, logistics, and supply chain management are dealt with in the next chapter.

Every department should consider quality metrics and each department should perform its function in a "quality" way. What does this mean? It means that every department should:

- Be customer-focussed, whether for internal or external customers;

- Be looking for continual improvement in how it performs;

- Be monitoring its performance and asking for feedback from internal and external customers;

- Aim for zero defects (i.e., zero times when internal and external customers are not happy, zero times when they have to repeat a process step, or zero times when they have to apologize to an internal or external customer);

- Aim to simplify its processes.

Why would we not apply this to all departments? It would improve our organization's performance, including its financial performance. And we don't need to employ expensive consultants to do this; we just need to use our quality personnel as internal consultants. Let's take a look at some specific departments.

Operations

Operations (also called Manufacturing or Production) is traditionally the realm in which the Quality department operates. But I'm suggesting that since quality can have an overarching impact on an organization, it should be considered to be outside of the Operations department. If Quality is kept within Operations, it will only have an effect *on* Operations.

Plenty has been written, and continues to be written, about the relationship between Quality and the Operations department. Rather than repeat the old arguments about conflicts between the two departments, I will just say this:

> The Quality department must demonstrate what it can contribute and how it can help Operations. This should be done in measures that mean something to Operations. It's not enough to say "The internal audits are behind schedule," or "You need to go look for that calibrated tool that's gone missing," or "This happened last month and now we have another complaint."

The Quality department should be saying things like this (using the same examples quoted above):

- "Delayed audits prevent us from demonstrating that we are doing what we say we are doing. Performing these audits gives us confidence that we are operating as we should and that we are not leaving ourselves exposed to unnecessary and potentially expensive risk. Audits not only help prevent problems, but they raise issues that will help us improve systems and processes. Although they are an organization tool and a requirement of certification, their real worth is in helping you run your department better."

- "If we cannot locate that tool when we need it, we could end up using a tool that is not calibrated. Any measurements taken with the substitute tool could be wrong. The consequence of this (for critical tools) might be the need for a recall for product that is with our customers. Even without the external consequence, we should not be satisfied that tools go missing. Lost tools create the need to buy a replacement (at a cost to the Operations department)."

- "The action we took last time was not effective. This complaint will cost us $x in terms of accepting the bad product, sorting it, reworking it, shipping it back on expedited freight, scrapping some product, rescheduling (with possible knock-on delays for other customers), and remaking product on overtime rates. Bad product quality will affect negotiations when it comes to renewing our contract with the customer. Let's set up a meeting where we can review the previous actions taken and the current complaint. I have some ideas that can help."

It is not enough for QA to present a weekly or monthly trend of nonconformances and tell Operations to sort it out. Although Operations may be responsible for some or most of it, and thus should be the ones driving the actions, QA can be a great resource, and this is how they should be viewed. On the other side, Operations and other departments should not use this as an opportunity to dump issues onto QA. Operations should ask the Quality department for their contribution in problem solving and continual improvement, while at the same time acknowledging that they are responsible for what they produce. This doesn't mean that they are necessarily responsible for the issues raised, which could be due to such things as faulty components, poor training, unrealistic deadlines, old equipment, inadequate specifications from the customer, or insufficient tooling. But Operations should be the driver. They are ones who are being directly affected by the issue. Operations should ensure that other departments take the appropriate actions, because Operations are the core of a manufacturing business, and other departments must support them. Operations usually carry the cost for bad quality product, so it is in their interest to ensure issues are properly resolved.

High-level quality KPIs for Operations could include:

- The number of parts shipped (A) minus the number of parts rejected internally (B) and minus the number of parts rejected by the customer (C). For service organizations, substitute the number of transactions for the number of parts shipped, and the number of complaints for the number of products.

- The cost of rework.

- The cost of sorting due to poor quality of manufacture.

- The cost of repairs due to poor quality of manufacture.

- The cost of having to make something a second time and the associated opportunity cost.

Design

I would argue that designers have more of an influence on product quality than any other department. It is critical that everyone in a design department understand that quality starts with them. If a designer does not design a good quality output (drawing, program, specification, model, prototype, service), people further down the chain will be left to pick up the pieces, dealing with issues that will exist until they are designed out. The other consequence is that the organization will end up having to employ more support people (quality engineers, manufacturing engineers, technicians, tech support personnel, and helpline representatives) to deal with issues that are beyond the control of those support people. Many organizations seem to have difficulty in grasping this concept. Quality, Engineering, Production and Service personnel need to be involved at the early stages of new product development, and need to remain as key members of the team during development.

> **Product and service quality is largely determined by the design department.**

All designers need to be trained in design for manufacture (DFM), design for use, design for servicing, design for installation, and design for test.

DFM includes such things as minimizing the number of parts required, modular assembly, using standard parts where possible, and reducing the number of operations required for assembly.

Each of these areas needs careful consideration to ensure that the concerns and demands of all design department customers are addressed as much as possible. Usually there will be compromises, but in a good design department, these become known items before the product leaves their department and are communicated to the various users in advance.

Doing a design and getting feedback is an iterative process, with the objective of optimizing the outcome. In my experience, there can be a tendency for designers to work in isolation, meaning there is insufficient communication with other departments. How often does your R&D department meet with Purchasing, Operations, Quality, Manufacturing Support, Sales and Marketing, Planning, and Logistics? These departments contribute greatly to improving the design of a product or service.

In fairness to R&D, there is a concern that any meeting held with other departments will generate more and more suggestions, resulting in either redesign or delay while discussions continue about whether to implement the changes suggested. But design changes should be explained to Sales and Marketing, just as market feedback should be shared with R&D.

What I propose is that the balance is too much in the R&D court. Even things like interdepartmental briefings or Failure Modes and Effects Analysis (FMEA) meetings can be ways of addressing the communication shortfall without overburdening R&D. They still have a product to design and a timescale in which to deliver it.

Other departments should, I would suggest, also be more involved with R&D. For instance, the Finance department could train project managers in how best to cost their project and prepare business plans. This could include looking at return on investment (ROI), payback period, net present value (NPV), and cashflow analysis.

From a departmental point of view, design metrics can sometimes be more difficult to work with than production metrics. Design departments are seen as black holes where only the "initiated" (i.e., those with design knowledge and experience) can question how things are done and under what timescales they run. When a change is requested by another department, it can be hard to get a date when the revised design or drawing will be ready. A lot of things may need to be checked and tested before a revised drawing is issued, but this should not absolve the design department from providing a reasonable completion date. Most designs are engineering rather than creative in nature, so it should be possible to estimate times required for each part of a design review or a testing program.

How should we measure the quality of output from a design department? Measuring the volume of output is not enough. Is it more relevant to measure the number and frequency of revisions? While this might sound like a good idea, we need to consider what is behind the changes. Maybe a customer or other user keeps requesting changes; in this case, it is beyond the control of the designers. This metric could still be used, identifying the number of changes due to requests originating outside R&D. We could ignore changes made before the product is officially released and only measure the number of changes requested after release. This can be useful to see where the origin of change requests lies. It's also possible to separate change requests into priority categories and then measure change implementation against a set timescale. We might have urgent "A" level changes with an implementation target of days or weeks; non critical "B" changes that have a longer implementation timeframe; and "C" level changes that are "nice to have" and implemented only when other higher level changes are going through at the same time or when that component is being modified. Making these kinds of classifications clear and posting status and due dates in an accessible location can remove some of the bad feeling that other departments have in relation to the design department. The lack of timescales can be a major frustration for them.

We understand in manufacturing or in service that if a problem is not found early on, the cost to fix it will increase as it progresses through the various processes. If there is a faulty component, we need to detect it as early as possible. Otherwise, we could end up having to scrap or rework a completed product, which is more expensive in terms of material and labor. If that fault is not detected within the organization, we could have defective products in the market, resulting in a possible recall situation. The same applies in design; a faulty calculation or dimension or assumption that is not detected immediately can have huge cost implications later on.

So how good are our systems in R&D to detect these issues?

Management can help by ensuring that designers get close to customers or users (including the organization's own manufacturing and service personnel) and that their requirements and limitations are understood. A user requirement specification (URS) may be used to clearly show customer requirements and expectations. Sometimes a functional requirement specification (FRS) is also generated, depending on the nature of the business. An FRS should give clear performance and quality standards and leave as little room as possible for ambiguity. A typical URS and FRS would contain things such as these:

- User interface requirements
- A description of the required system performance
- Performance criteria, critical parameters, operating range
- Maintenance requirements
- Any regulatory requirements
- Documentation requirements
- Training requirements

Although a URS or FRS might be too extreme for many organizations, a checklist of the standard user requirements should be considered (some version of this may already be in place). This ensures that key process steps in bringing in a new or modified product are not overlooked.

Where there is often a gap, though, is in the organization's own manufacturing and service capabilities. A checklist is also required so that production/service and quality personnel can have a say in how a product is to be manufactured. This is key to reaching the productivity levels that are needed in today's business environment, and should not be ignored.

It's important to re-emphasise that quality of design refers to service as well as to product. Organizations can have both aspects, where they perform after-sales support, maintenance, or installation.

The design department can, in many organizations, be responsible for feeding information to Sales and Marketing in terms of what product options are available and what options are compatible or incompatible. Supplying incorrect information can generate extra work to "force" a particular option to work. Most organizations do not like going back to a customer to say that they made a mistake and the option requested is not available.

Another potential weak spot for R&D is not having a process in place to keep track of "lessons learned." It's important to keep track of solutions that have or have not worked particularly well (in production or in the field), or where feedback is received by the Sales and Marketing or Quality departments. This will help prevent similar problems from happening in the future. Sometimes, the lessons learned system only exists in someone's head based on previous experience, and this is far from a satisfactory situation. Weaknesses identified in previous products or services must not be allowed to appear in new products or services.

Finally, do we identify the critical characteristics/parameters/ dimensions/performance requirements in our specifications and drawings? It is obvious that we should. This allows our suppliers to ensure that the critical areas receive the most attention.

Engineering

Engineering departments in various organizations perform very different functions. Broadly speaking, Engineering is the department responsible for the site/facility and equipment, including such things as preventive maintenance, infrastructure (lighting, HVAC, utility supplies), capital equipment, and potentially capability studies on equipment. Some organizations have a Manufacturing Engineering or Production Engineering department, which may or may not fall under the Engineering department. Obviously if these are included, other items fall within the scope of the Engineering department, such as developing work instructions, specifying equipment for manufacture and test, laying out the Production area.

The Engineering department plays a key role in determining the quality of what is produced by an organization, responsible for the specification and capability of machinery versus the tolerances required on a product, how well equipment is maintained, lighting for visual inspection or camera inspection, preventive maintenance, calibration and repair of equipment, the availability of spare parts, and machine reliability.

If equipment is purchased solely by price, without regard to product specifications, there will be continual added cost to the organization by virtue of regular tweaking of machinery in order to produce product that is in spec. This will include the cost of additional maintenance, more spare parts, extra inspection time and personnel for suspect product, and extra engineers and technicians. It is false economy to purchase equipment solely on price. If a piece of machinery is more costly, you can depreciate its cost over time; but if you end up with extra inspection and personnel, this will be a continual, and increasing, cost over the lifetime of the equipment (due to increasing payroll costs over time and necessary repairs and adjustments needed for aging machinery. When submitting capex budgets, it's important to consider these factors and estimate cost associated with each one over the life of the equipment.

Equipment capability and reliability are absolutely essential prerequisites if an organization wants to go the "lean" route—reducing work in progress (WIP), just in time (JIT), and deliveries to customers. If this cannot be demonstrated (by capability studies, reliability studies, and preventive maintenance records), then "lean" should not be implemented; it will fail due to unscheduled equipment failure and product manufactured outside specification.

The Engineering department can also sometimes be the department that puts bills of materials (BOMs) up on an organization's computer system. In my experience, BOMs often contain errors, especially as a product goes through revision changes. These errors can be large where the incorrect quantity is specified on a BOM or the description is not exact enough, causing the purchasing department to order a similar but incorrect part or a part of inferior specification. It can save time in the long run to have someone verify the BOMs are correct. In some engineering software, the BOM is generated automatically from the CAD data, which may obviate the need for this check. The same format should be used for part numbering and part descriptions.

It would also be nice if part numbering and part descriptions followed a consistent approach.

An associated area of responsibility for Engineering is setting the times for each step of the process. The times that are entered onto a system are used when summarizing the number of products made divided by the total number of hours worked and the hourly rates. An incorrect time, especially if it's underestimated, can make a product or service seem (more) profitable when this may not be the case. Conversely, it can show a product as being unprofitable when, in fact, it may be OK to go ahead with it.

Timings are also used by Production departments to monitor productivity rates. It is easy to see how errors in the system can create erroneous reports of productivity. Even if such an error is detected, people may not want to change it for fear of the metric changing significantly from the previous month (where a good trend suddenly shows a dip in the wrong direction), so the error continues. This is as much a cultural issue as an Engineering one; if people are afraid of admitting a mistake, an organization can continue thinking a particular product or service is generating profit, when in fact it is not. The Finance department will be scratching their heads trying to figure out why things are not adding up, and the longer the error goes unreported, the bigger the potential loss to the organization.

Sales and Marketing

How can Sales and Marketing impact quality in your organization? The following items can affect product or service quality:

- The lead time promised for products or services, especially new or revised ones.

- Standard or customized options. There is always a tendency to say "yes" when a customer asks for something different, but a particular option may not be possible even though it looks possible on paper. Even if it is possible, a particular option may fall foul of regulatory or environmental restrictions, or may incur excessive manufacturing or test costs.

- The lead time for after-sales products. In my experience, after-sales products are rarely costed properly. These products can sometimes be fully or partially handmade, assembled, or tested and these extra costs may not be included in the price. The material may be costed correctly, but invariably the time cost is significantly underestimated (often based on the time for producing a part on the production line). Organizations may decide this is just the cost of doing business, but costs add up if the amount of after-sales support required is high. We may have to keep stock of unique components to satisfy the after-sales market, and there is a cost associated with this. There may also be increased purchasing costs of unique components (where we now only wish to purchase one hundred per year instead of ten thousand). After-sales multiplier factors should be included in the original contract to minimize any potential losses.

- Quotations. If quotes are inaccurate or incorrect, we could end up providing products or services at a loss or not covering all our bases. This can result in the organization being exposed to product or service risks, or having to pay for extra costs that were not addressed properly in the quote. The system should be set up to prevent the quotation being submitted if any item is not addressed. In the digital age, this is quite easy to do; there is really no excuse for key risk areas being overlooked in submitting quotations to customers.

Sales and Marketing can also feed back vital information from the market in terms of:

- Which products are performing well, and which aren't
- What customers are saying about a product or service
- What new products, features, or services are being asked for by customers
- Where customers see opportunities for future products or services

Is there a channel or forum for these messages to be fed back to the Design department? Why is feedback from Sales and Marketing sometimes ignored by Design departments or by senior managers? Surely they are (along with Quality) representing the voice of the customer (VOC) and thus should be taken more seriously? Sales and Marketing can be the first to become aware of potential issues in the market, even before the Quality department have started receiving complaints, so we should be utilizing this early warning system.

What system(s) do we have in place to disseminate information and ensure issues are properly addressed? I have seen organizations where the Sales or Marketing people gave up reporting issues back to Design or to other managers because nothing was being done to fix the issues. There can be many good reasons for not taking action on certain things, but it's crucial to communicate that back to the originator of the request.

Finance

Traditionally, the Quality and Finance departments have not had many dealings with each other except at budget time. Things have started to improve, and there is now one major tool that links these departments—the cost of quality (sometimes called the cost of poor quality). This tool is well developed, and breaks down quality-related costs into four major categories:

1. Prevention costs—the costs involved with putting in place systems, tools, and resources to prevent problems occurring. Typical items include supplier evaluation and audits, quality plans, process capability analysis, failure mode and effects analysis (FMEA), quality improvement projects, error proofing, quality training, and education.

2. Appraisal costs—the costs associated with making sure the product or service is as planned. In manufacturing, inspection is the usual example of this type of cost. Inspection is how most organizations determine whether a product is OK or not, but it does not add any value. Customer surveys are another type of appraisal cost, as are calibration, and incoming inspection.

3. Internal rejection costs—the cost of scrapping a part, the cost of sorting parts, the cost of reworking parts, and the cost of doing a job again. Internal rejection costs could also include expedited shipping due to quality issues, downgrading of product, and scrapping obsolete components or product.

4. External rejection costs—the costs associated with customer complaints, regulatory failure, litigation, sales discounts due to sub-standard product or service, product recall costs, warranty costs, and opportunity costs.

Apart from the above, there is a move toward involving the Finance department when it comes to justifying quality-related projects, e.g., Six Sigma projects. The Finance department will also play a key role in organizations where Sarbanes-Oxley (SOx) compliance is a requirement.

If the Quality department wants to be taken more seriously by senior management, then it needs to work with Finance to show the financial benefits of its proposals. This might include things such as moving to a different supplier (where the extra cost of the piece price is more than offset by the reduction in inspection, scrap, rework, and supplier related costs), investing in more fool-proof technology (that reduces human error), and changing a component (to reduce customer complaints). Some projects can be hard to justify in ROI terms, but might still be justified in terms of either the costs that will be avoided by implementing the project, or the risks to the organization if nothing is done. And then there are those times when money must be spent to comply with regulations, or where certification is necessary in order to generate business.

Human Resources

How might Human Resources and Quality interact? Well, when HR go looking for people, do they use trustworthy and reliable recruitment organizations, do they follow up on references, do they check the validity of a candidate's certificates or experience, do they keep accurate records? How do they ensure that they are in compliance with relevant data protection legislation? How are performance appraisals structured to prevent bias and avoid putting people from other cultures at a disadvantage? If an employee has a grievance, how quickly do HR sort it out and do they check back with the employee to ensure that the issue has been resolved satisfactorily?

Another area worthy of mention is that of incentives and bonuses. Do HR drive the right behavior, and not just in the short term?

At a more strategic level, HR can influence quality by ensuring that only those candidates with the right attitude are brought into the organization. As mentioned elsewhere, certain skills can be taught, but if someone does not have a "quality" attitude, then no amount of coaching will change that. That hire will be an expensive mistake. It makes more financial sense to spend time and perhaps money up front, to ensure that the right people are recruited. It is analogous to the previous discussion where R&D designs a sub-standard product and the organization has to live with the consequences.

A further area that often comes under HR is that of training. How is training set up? Is a gap analysis performed? Is it done for all levels of the organization? Does a matrix exist showing the level of cross-training? (This is usually done only for production operators.)

Finally, succession planning is an area where HR is involved. Although we tend to think of this in terms of management, it can be just as important in other key roles. For example, if we rely on one mechanical or one electrical designer, what are the risks if that person leaves? We need to look at all roles where there is only one person performing a particular task or where there is a specialist role (e.g., SOx compliance, standards compliance, shipment paperwork).

IT

Quality departments often have specialized QMS software or document management systems, and IT can be a key partner in ensuring these run smoothly. IT will be the ones setting up access to the software, and must ensure that it does not conflict with (or duplicate) existing software.

IT is involved in terms of the storage of inspection or audit records, setting up password controls, and ensuring the ERP system is functioning correctly.

ISO auditors often ask about an organization's procedure for system backups and the whole area of risk management in relation to IT because organizations are reliant on computer systems. Have you discussed what would happen if the IT system were to go down for more than a few hours? Do you know what backup or hardware duplication is in place? How would you contact employees, suppliers, or customers if all those details were only available on the computer system? This forms part of "business continuity planning," where an organization looks at the potential risks to its ability to operate. Does your organization have a business continuity plan? If not, I would suggest you put one in place. If you have one, how often is it reviewed? Who is involved in the review? Are senior managers involved? What are the results of such a review? ISO standard 22301 for business continuity planning can help in formulating such a plan, and there are also many resources available online.

The centralizing of the IT support function within organizations happened quickly, and sometimes it seems that IT departments have suffered under the pressure of centralized metrics.

Previously, if people had an issue they would call to the local IT person and ask for help, but now it's often a case of "raise a ticket or service request." Visibility is often lost from the user's perspective. There may be an automated mail to say the issue is acknowledged or is being dealt with, but the user is not, in my experience, given a timeframe for when it will be investigated or resolved. This creates frustration for the user. What we find is that the priority for dealing with issues is now being driven by the IT department, not by the needs of the user or the business. This is not a criticism of the people working in IT, but I contend that the move to raise tickets and service requests is an example of where metric-driven management has created another casualty in the law of unintended consequences. The end result is that IT end up as if they are the customer, and users must wait until their ticket is next in the queue. It seems like another inward departmental focus instead of an internal customer focus. This is typical of centralized departments in large organizations. So although we may be maximizing the efficiency of IT, this approach could be having serious efficiency effects on other departments. Is this the way we want it to work? Is this the best way, when we look at the organization as a whole? Let us at least be brave enough to ask the questions— of all centralized departments.

IT responsibilities are growing year on year. They are now involved with SOx compliance, data protection (both organization and personal), and virus/spam/hacking/malware protection. They ensure software is legitimate and that licences are up to date, prevent unauthorized access to computer systems, prevent users from loading files or programs that could endanger the security of the system or leave the organization exposed to licensing issues, and prevent users or competitors from stealing sensitive organization data.

These are all critical issues for an organization, and defined procedures need to be in place to deal with them.

Purchasing, Logistics, and Supply Chain Management

This is covered separately in the next chapter.

CHAPTER SUMMARY

In this chapter we made the case for every department to operate in a "quality" way, and we then went on to show what this means for various departments.

Questions

1. What is the relationship in your organization between Quality and R&D? Does R&D share information well? Are Quality and Production involved in new or modified designs at an early stage?

2. Do the technical departments meet regularly with Sales and Marketing to explain new or modified designs? Do Sales and Marketing people explain market and customer information to the technical departments?

3. Does the Finance department conduct training sessions with other departments on how to produce a mini business plan and fully costed proposals, so that such plans have a better chance of succeeding?

4. What information do you give to HR in terms of the attitude of the person for which you are recruiting? Do you over-rely on the job spec at the expense of the person spec?

5. How well is IT regarded in your organization? Do users get a chance to express their satisfaction?

CHAPTER TEN

✳ ✳ ✳

Quality and Suppliers, Logistics, and Supply Chain Management

CHAPTER OUTLINE:

In this chapter we look at supplier agreements and contracts, supplier categories, and supplier selection and then review some specific aspects of the supplier relationship—purchasing, goods-in, material storage, and supplier monitoring and development. I have given this its own chapter because for many organizations, suppliers significantly affect final product or service quality.

Most organizations have suppliers and customers, and when thinking about how to look at our suppliers, we can sometimes learn a lot from how our customers deal with us. We should always be on the lookout for better ways of doing things. For example, I have used the "5 whys" approach to identifying the root cause of problems for many years. Some time ago a supplier sent in a version of a 5 whys document I had not seen before. Their approach made a lot of sense, and I made a note of it for future use. Similarly, I have seen many examples of procedures or FMEA documents over the years and have modified some to use in my organization.

Some organizations seem to view suppliers almost as a necessary evil, and try to squeeze as much as possible out of them. This is a blinkered approach. We are suppliers to our customers; would we like them to treat us in the same way we treat our suppliers? In an ideal world, we would like to have several customers, allowing us freedom to terminate an agreement with any one of them if the terms and conditions did not suit us. In a world where growth is a key measure of success, this does not happen often, even when it means huge extra (and often hidden) costs that must be absorbed by the organization (e.g., where there is customization of a product or service required, and we agree to do it for free or for a fixed price, or where we accept a low price in order to win more business or to continue doing business with that customer). We need to keep these thoughts in mind when dealing with our own suppliers. Are they too reliant on us, or is that a concern? Do they say "yes" to everything?

Most organizations have various types of suppliers, from critical to incidental. A typical way to deal with this is to view them in categories. This is illustrated in Figure 13.

For category C suppliers, there will probably be no need to inspect items or verify the service received; there may not be a contract. If there is a contract, it will be less stringent than those for category A or B suppliers. For category A suppliers, there is often a contract (see possible clauses below), there may be standards or specifications for inspecting the parts delivered with agreed acceptance/rejection criteria, we might only deal with organizations certified to ISO 9001, and we may request additional test and inspection data.

A supplier agreement is an essential document in most organizations for dealing with key suppliers. One key thing that those writing contracts should keep in mind is that contracts should reflect what is being supplied according to the potential risk to your organization. We do not need a detailed contract for an item or service that is of low value or low volume and one that does not have a significant impact on the final product or service.

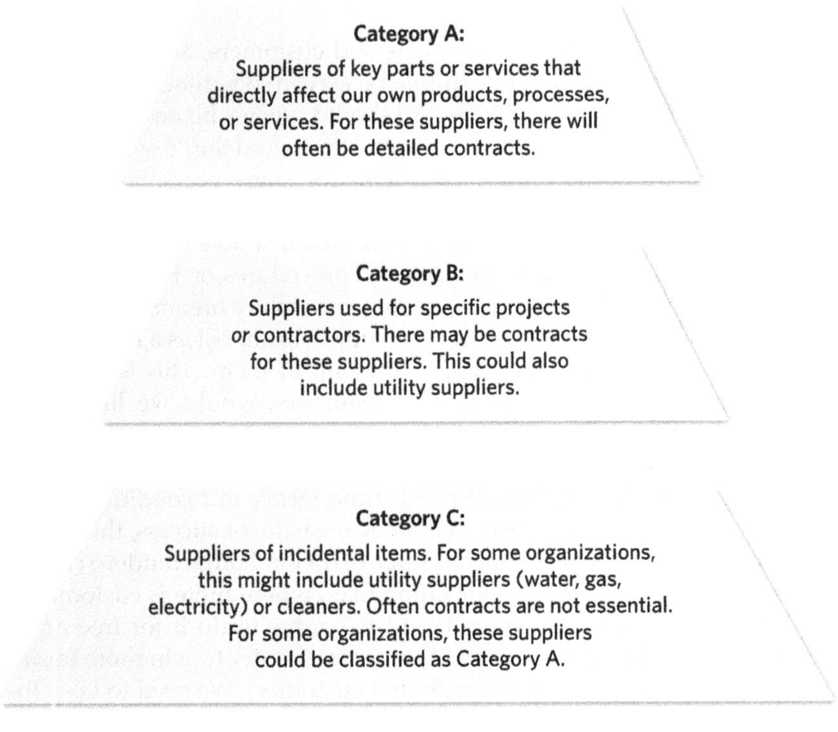

Category A:
Suppliers of key parts or services that directly affect our own products, processes, or services. For these suppliers, there will often be detailed contracts.

Category B:
Suppliers used for specific projects or contractors. There may be contracts for these suppliers. This could also include utility suppliers.

Category C:
Suppliers of incidental items. For some organizations, this might include utility suppliers (water, gas, electricity) or cleaners. Often contracts are not essential. For some organizations, these suppliers could be classified as Category A.

Figure 13 Supplier categories.

If you do not have such a contract already, sample contracts can be found online, or your customer may have a supplier contract with you that can be adapted for use with your suppliers.

A contract will usually include items such as these:

- A minimum contract length

  Contracts often have a yearly or multi-year rollover (the latter being more applicable for high-cost items or projects). Suppliers want as long a contract as possible, while customers often want the opposite because it gives them more flexibility. As a customer, we need to give our key suppliers the comfort of knowing they can depend on us ordering parts from them (as long as price, quality, and delivery conform to any agreements made between the two parties); this also helps build up the relationship and trust between the organizations. It is in our interest as a customer to keep that relationship and trust going, and it's important to remember that how we treat our suppliers can affect our own reputation. As a quid pro quo, our suppliers should be willing to share relevant new developments, be open to cost reduction projects, and as treat problems quickly and seriously. The length of a contract is often affected by the level of investment required by the supplier, because the supplier needs to recoup its investment in tooling or equipment or offices or warehouses, etc.

- Orders
  - Minimum order quantity (MOQ): The MOQ is often related to price, though not in every case. We should do our own costings with our finance department to see which is better for us—to order large volumes at lower cost (and factor in the cost of storage and possible expiration or obsolescence), or to go with a higher cost for smaller volumes. Sometimes the decision can be down to the attitude of senior management about risk, though we can minimize that risk by having more than one supplier for any one part or service. Of course, this brings in another factor. Having more than one supplier means we have to manage and measure those extra suppliers and the prices we pay can be higher because we are now ordering less from a single supplier. As with many things, trying to solve one problem can raise other issues.

  - Order frequency and method: Will we cut individual purchase orders or place orders by means of a schedule?

- Minimum stocking levels: Is there an agreement for the supplier to keep a certain quantity of stock (either all parts or just critical or big parts) in their warehouse, or at a location nearby, or in our warehouse? This can help us minimize stock as well as give a level of confidence if a batch is rejected or we get an urgent order. Of course, we must guarantee that we will purchase any stock they have if parts (components or semi-finished or finished product) become obsolete or changed in such a way that the older version cannot be used, or the supplier is left with stock because of the minimum order quantity requirement. This is often referred to as an O and E clause (obsolete and excess); we need to balance the value and volume of stock held versus the Planning department's desire to prevent running out of stock.

- For service- or project-related contracts: We need specific monitoring stages—gates or handover points—with agreed criteria as to what should the "output" at each stage. Output could be a drawing, a calculation, a costed proposal, a specification, a Gantt chart, or perhaps the project itself has defined stages.

• Quality

We need to set and agree to key performance indicators in relation to quality, delivery, and service. This could include the maximum number of rejects allowed (possibly categorized into critical, major, or minor), number of supplier corrective action requests (SCARS), any audits to be undertaken and the consequences of unacceptable results, and the consequences for failing to meet the agreed KPIs. (Note: If a SCAR/8D comes back from a supplier saying the corrective/preventive action is "more training" or the cause is shown as "human error," this generally is not an acceptable response. Humans make mistakes, so the quality system must be designed to eliminate human error. If it can't eliminate mistakes, the supplier needs to specify how they will detect the error in-house before delivery; training can be vague or insufficient; how does a supplier ensure that anyone transferring to that area or new to that area will have the appropriate training)?

- Cost of defective items or service: Will the supplier issue replacement parts free of charge or issue a credit, or do we withhold payment?

- Cost of removing faulty parts from a line, or costs that are incurred when faulty parts have gone to our customer: Most suppliers will only agree to cover the cost of their own defective parts. Consequential costs and losses is a legal area and proper legal advice is needed. In any event, what do you do if the supplier does not accept such costs?

- Agreed sorting process: Who pays, who carries out the sorting (the supplier, us, an outside organization), who is responsible for rework cost rates, labor rates (whether us or an outside organization)?

- Cost of contacting customers to re-supply parts or re-supply the service.

- Possible admin fee for complaints, i.e., a minimum set cost for dealing with each complaint, irrespective of the final cost.

- Incentives for good quality: This could include inviting people to our site, showing them around, and paying for dinner/hotel; it could take the form of a change to the terms and conditions, it could be the early confirmation of the renewal of a contract, or it could be the extension of a contract.

- Quality improvement targets.

- Supplier to send final inspection and/or final test data on a periodic basis. This could also apply to other key steps in the supplier's process. Statistical process control (SPC) data, capability study results data, validation results, and other trend data would be particularly useful to receive, and would give us more confidence in their processes.

- Packaging
  - Dimensions and weights of pallets and boxes.
  - Recommended storage conditions and disposal.
  - Packaging—quantity of product per box.
  - The number of boxes per pallet.
  - Labelling requirements—what information should be on the label and in what format (human readable, 1D or 2D barcode, barcode standard to be used).
  - Maximum height of a pallet.
  - Maximum weight of a pallet (can pallets be stacked; can boxes be stacked).
  - Maximum weight of one box.

- Wrapping to be used.
- Wooden packaging (including wooden pallets) must be treated wood and must be marked to provide evidence of this.
- Is the packaging to be collapsible or returnable?
- Defined carton size.
- Packaging labels must have our part number on it as well as theirs; labels must show the description and rev number of the part, and traceability information (time, date, lot number, or batch code).
- Where possible, packaging should be in a shape and quantity that can go straight to the line without decanting.
- Where financially beneficial (i.e., for high-value or critical items), supplier to put a radio frequency identification (RFID) tag on the products or the product containers supplied.
- Special labels to be applied when new or modified or screened product is being delivered (e.g., after a SCAR has been issued). We also need to agree for how many deliveries the new labels must be applied.
- For custom parts (i.e., parts specifically designed for our product), all changes must be approved in writing by us before the supplier has the authority to produce or ship parts to us. In emergencies, we might allow a supplier to "build at risk" or "ship at risk" in order to minimize the risk to ourselves of being late with our shipments.

- Other questions
  - Who pays for expedited freight where a delivery or service is late or falls below the agreed quality level?
  - What type of forms will be used? Do we want suppliers to use our CAR (corrective action request) form or can they use their own? Are electronic forms acceptable? Are electronic signatures acceptable?
  - What about supplier audits—frequency, product, and process audits? Should we ask for the ability to do unannounced audits?
  - What penalty will apply if a supplier fails to notify us of a product change (including all revision changes)? We might include a clause that says we will move them from "certified" status to "conditional" status if this happens.
  - Will we include cost improvement targets?

- What number of cost saving projects will be proposed;

- What notification do we require if the supplier wishes to change anything about the product or service (sub-supplier, material, process, new or different equipment, different operators, different logistics company)?

- How are changes to be communicated between us and the supplier? Are there agreed forms, do we require written acknowledgment that the changes have been received and accepted? Do we require the first deliveries to be specially identified in some way?

We can add any number of clauses and end up with a 500-page document, but ultimately our relationship with suppliers must be built on trust. Few organizations can place a full-time person in a supplier's site. Even if that were financially viable, could we afford to do it for all critical suppliers?

Supplier Selection

How often do we get situations where an organization says "we will pick our suppliers based on quality, price, and delivery," or "based on the input of all departments" (Purchasing, Quality, Engineering), but ends up choosing the cheapest supplier? This only serves to de-motivate other departments and everyone can clearly see that the organization is ultimately interested in the cheapest source. But like buying cheap machinery, is buying the cheapest components the best option in the long run? It may well be, but it should not be an automatic assumption. We must consider what might be the associated costs if this supplier started sending in defective material, had a strike in its factory, could not deliver due to transportation issues, fell behind in deliveries, or went out of business. Of course, these questions apply to any potential supplier, but often the cheapest supplier is located in a different continent. This causes additional issues:

- It is harder to get a picture on the ground of day-to-day operations.

- We are more susceptible to expensive transport costs if a shipment is missed.

- There is a foreign exchange risk.

- The relationship may not be not as strong because of fewer face-to-face meetings and possible language differences.

- Changes may take longer to implement because of the longer pipeline of product.

- There may be a long lead time to get replacements. If we try to circumvent this by having extra stock closer to our site, this has cost implications.

- The time difference may result in limited times when both parties are available to discuss issues by phone or video conference.

- There may be other costs—transport, extra packaging, extra insurance, the increase in lead time, any delays due to misunderstandings or misinterpretations of requests. There may be customs costs, potential reliability costs due to using a supplier not be as technically competent as an organization closer to home, supplier audits than would be the case for home-based suppliers, and the loss of intellectual property.

- There may be more inspection costs.

- Other departments such as Production, Engineering, or Quality may have to shoulder extra costs because more jigs are required, more on-line inspection is required, more employees are required, a separate rework area may be required.

There is a case to be made for getting a landed price for a part from a cheaper, off-shore potential supplier and then revisiting existing or potential suppliers nearer home to see how close they can get to this price. It need not be the same price due to the costs noted above, as these would not apply to a home-based supplier. But by adopting this approach, we might create a virtuous circle. Because we buy from closer to home, more jobs are created or retained, and the long-term stability and viability of the supplier is improved. This is, of course, assuming that quality, price, and delivery are comparable to similar products on the market.

We need to be fair to all departments; if we're going to go for the cheapest supplier, we should inform all departments that this is the driving criteria. And businesses should properly cost the risks associated with far away suppliers before making a decision. Too often the justification for a cheap supplier only considers the piece price.

Do other departments really have a say in choosing a supplier? I have seen many instances where the rhetoric might indicate the valued input of all relevant departments, but reality is that either:

- Once R&D have found a source, that supplier may be the only source for that part and therefore it doesn't really matter what other departments think, or

- Purchasing will propose the cheapest supplier and it can be hard to argue against that, because many of the costs listed above are unknown at the time.

Once we have defined supplier selection criteria and supplier evaluation criteria, we can start evaluating possible sources.

When choosing a supplier, it is normal to look at a number of factors and perform a number of due diligence steps:

- Determining financial status
- Requesting financial references from their bank
- Verifying tax compliance
- Checking customer references addressing reliability and responsiveness
- Viewing their product or trialling their service
- Looking at their history
- Asking what investment or new products or services they are planning
- Meeting their managers
- Conducting a supplier quality audit
- Getting a picture for how the supplier is viewed in the market
- Finding out the market share of the supplier
- Asking the supplier to highlight strengths (their differentiators) and weaknesses
- Evaluating contractor qualifications and appropriate insurance coverage
- Depending on the product, having samples independently tested to ensure they conform to relevant specifications and standards
- Meeting with their technical people to see what level of support can be given
- Benchmarking their product or service against similar ones in the market

But we also need to know our potential suppliers in terms of their capabilities, quality levels, lead times, and prices.

When a selection is almost made, it can be worth asking for details of the supplier's SPC data or other data that show the variation in their manufacturing processes. This will be a good indicator of how often we might expect to see suspect or defective product leaving their premises.

We may also have a requirement for our suppliers to conform to best practices in terms of corporate social responsibility guidelines, health and safety regulations, child labor, hazardous materials, and environmental responsibility, and conformance to quality specifications. We may want to formalize this by saying that any potential suppliers must be certified to the various international standards, but we should make our own initial assessment of these areas. We can use the certification from a third party also, but there is no substitute for seeing a supplier's processes first hand.

Purchasing

Do we ensure that purchase orders (POs) are authorized before sending to suppliers? This needs to be done to prevent fraud and it's a requirement in some quality standards. Only certain roles should be authorized to generate or process POs, and each role should have a limit in terms of what value people in that position can order. This is often presented as a matrix, showing the role versus the authorisation limit of a PO, but we need to also consider how we hardwire this into our software. It is nice to be able to show a matrix, but the important thing is how this requirement is implemented and enforced. We need to be sure that people cannot exceed their purchasing authority. It would be normal for two or more documented approvals to be required before approving larger value orders. How do we ensure and demonstrate that two people review all POs, or at least all POs over a certain value? How do we implement these controls when people use company credit cards for online purchases?

When we prepare our POs for production parts, we should include the following:

- The part number (ours and the suppliers, if applicable), description, and revision number of the part.

- The standard or specification required (or reference to these). This could also include a requirement that the supplier must be ISO 9001 certified, or that a contractor must have valid insurance and tax credentials, or that the product must meet certain product or industry standards.

- Our terms and conditions, which may include packaging requirements or refer to our standard purchasing agreement.

- Any quality requirements required (e.g., a certificate of conformance or certificate of analysis, the supplier's test, SPC, or final inspection results).

Receiving, Identification, and Storage

I am always surprised at the number of organizations where, after a shipment has arrived, proceed to relabel boxes and decant the delivery into other containers. A supplier agreement should cover labelling and packaging requirements. With the right labelling, the most an organization should have to do is to scan the parts into stock. Anything more than that is waste.

Is our system set up so that once a label is scanned, all the relevant information is put onto our system (PO number, quantity received, part number, description, part revision, date received, goods received note number, certificate of conformance number)? There should be no need for manual entry of data at goods-in, except for some specific circumstances (maybe a label or a box gets damaged, or the supplier sends in a partial shipment). If we do not perform any incoming inspection, then parts should be showing in stock within a few hours of receipt. Is this the case in our organizations? If we do perform inspection at goods-in, do we know why we are inspecting those items? Are the criteria still valid?

How do we identify parts that require inspection? The normal way is to use the enterprise resource planning (ERP) system to flag these parts so that they cannot be transferred into stock without sign-off (usually by Quality). Do we also put a label on such parts? Do we need to do this? Do we have specific locations for parts awaiting inspection? These are all ways to ensure that parts do not get transferred into stock without the required inspection.

For new or revised parts, do we ask the supplier to put a special label on packaging and a note on the paperwork? This should be done where we have a new supplier, where a new or revised part is being delivered, or where we have had a quality problem and the supplier is identifying the next few deliveries for inspection by us.

Incoming inspection, if performed at all, should be based on criticality/risk and on our historical results. We should not inspect everything just because that is what we have always done. Ultimately it goes back to trust in our suppliers. Do we believe they can consistently produce good quality items, or not? If we do, then why do we inspect, or at least inspect at our current level? If we don't believe it, then why do we continue to use them, and is the cost of this inspection reflected in the business case for continuing to use them (and was it included when the case was being made to select them in the first place)?

It could be argued that if we decide to go with the cheapest supplier and ignore their quality level, then the cost of the incoming inspection should come from the Purchasing department budget and not the Quality department budget. That might improve the focus on using high quality suppliers!

For many purchased components, it is useful to have a reference sample at goods-in with the part number, description, and revision level. If an actual sample part is not practical, then a 2D or 3D image or photo or drawing can be used. The part specification should also be available to the incoming inspection personnel and this might include cosmetic criteria. In some cases, we may have to send samples to a test house, if the characteristic cannot be inspected in-house. Or maybe we can rely on the test information provided by the supplier.

Parts should arrive into our warehouse in a manner that does not require us to decant them (i.e., transfer them from their packaging into containers suitable for our warehouse or production line). If we have or can create sufficient space on the line, we may even be able to store certain components only on the line and then there is no need to keep stock in the warehouse at all.

Traceability information is essential. All suppliers should put human-readable and 1D or 2D bar codes on their boxes including part number, revision number, lot/batch code or date code, customer part number, and customer revision number. Having the supplier put a loose traceability label in each box can be a big help if we discover a problem later on, especially where we keep that label with the parts when they are on the line. It is then easy to identify the faulty batch.

There should be periodic exercises carried out to look at tracing forwards and backwards. Tracing forwards is where we pick a component, identify its lot code or date code, and then go through our process identifying where that batch of components was used. Ideally, we would hope to be able to identify what finished goods products they were used on, and to whom they were sold and when. Tracing backwards is where we start with a finished goods product, identify its batch or date code (the one generated by us), and then see whether, by using this information, we can trace back to identify the batch or date code of one or more components used on that product.

Being able to trace components in both directions is very important. If a customer reports a serious issue (and for this exercise, we assume that the root cause of the problem is due to a faulty component), we need to be able to identify what other finished product might be affected and to whom it has been sold, because we may need to contact those customers to get the product returned. Alongside this, we need to continue tracing back so that we can identify the date or batch code of the faulty component. After that has been done, we then do our forward traceability to ensure we identify all finished product that is in the market or in our production that might have the same problem. Only at that stage can a discussion be held regarding the next step. Do we say and do nothing, or do we contact each customer individually and offer to send a free replacement? Do we put a notice on our website, or do we issue a product recall? We need to put a boundary around the problem in terms of being able to say "this is the total quantity of product that is or could be affected by this problem." Then management can make the final decision on what action is to be taken.

Stock rotation (first in, first out–FIFO), is also an issue. How do we ensure that we use the oldest parts first? Is our process robust enough to prevent people taking stock from the front of a rack or from another location? We can look at designing the warehouse to try to ensure this, but we should let the system control it (i.e., prevent newer stock from being withdrawn before older stock). This is usually done by scanning product out of stock, rather than manually keying in the information. If someone scans the part from a later date or from the wrong location, the system can alert or stop the release process until a supervisor or manager resets the alarm.

If we require extra traceability, we could ensure that the labels from our supplier have a unique sequential number on them and then log that number into our system, allowing the system to know which box number should be released next. Critical components may have their own unique serial number, which we can record in our system for enhanced traceability.

In a system of visual control for small items, the ideal would be to load received parts to the back of a rack and issue them from the front of a rack.

We should consider getting the supplier to put RFID (radio frequency identification) tags on all parts above a certain value or parts that are critical to our business. This would speed up locating such parts and maintain good traceability. RFID can also be used for finished product for tracking purposes. This can prove very useful when exporting high value items.

If you have a large warehouse, it might be worthwhile to ask how often parts cannot be found on time, and how much time is spent trying to locate them. Even with computerised systems, this issue still occurs. RFID can help here (if financially justifiable). Some organizations have a policy of having specific locations for specific part numbers, so that parts are always only in one place. This has a few advantages, but at least one disadvantage. Warehouse space may not be used efficiently, and we can end up with empty spaces in one area of the racking while other parts are stored on the floor because of a lack of space in another area. Why not at least have the discussion to see which option is best?

Agreement must be reached in terms of how we will control our stock. Will it be ship to stock (where the supplier's parts go straight into our warehouse without any inspection), Kanban (where the volume of stock is controlled by a physical or electronic Kanban card), or just in time (where the supplier has visibility of our stock levels and delivers parts only when they are needed)? We need to give careful consideration in how these are set up, and anticipate the implications if anything goes wrong once a process is in place. We also need to sit down with our suppliers to explain these systems, because they may not have used them with other customers. Even where they have used them before, there still needs to be discussion and agreement on the specifics of how we want to implement stock control. For example, if we implement Kanban, we need to agree on the restocking quantity, on how long the supplier has to supply stock, and on how the signal is given to the supplier—via Kanban card or email. If it is an email, we need to build in safeguards in relation to backup personnel. Who will handle things if the usual sender or receiver is sick or on holidays? What approximate time will the email will be sent, and what days? These safeguards allow the supplier to contact us if they have not received notification within the agreed timeframe.

Just in time (JIT) systems require significant planning by both organizations, and one key factor is equipment uptime. We need to be satisfied that the supplier has a rigorous preventive maintenance program for their equipment, and we may also require details of backup plans for times when key equipment breaks down, or the delivery truck breaks down, or there is a strike or a natural disaster. A lot of things can go wrong, and we need to assess each possibility against the likelihood and impact on us if any of them (or a combination of them) happens. For this reason, many organizations keep a minimum stock on hand. Before JIT, they might have kept up to three months stock or more; with JIT, they might keep four weeks or two days stock.

Some organizations use a nearby warehouse for most of their stock, and only keep enough on-site for one or two days. This can make the warehouse look very efficient, but it may not bring huge efficiencies or cost benefits overall. We will be paying for the other warehouse and we may have huge amounts of stock, but there is a danger that, because there is another warehouse, the Planners might simply proceed to fill it up, thus ensuring no stock-outs. There are some actions we can take to mitigate this (e.g., ask suppliers to manage their stock in that warehouse knowing we don't pay for it until it reaches our on-site warehouse), and we set maximum stock quantities of each part. We also need to have transport available to get the parts from the warehouse to the main site. So we need to be careful that we don't just move the inefficiencies from our own warehouse to the nearby warehouse—that is not addressing the real problem.

When you walk around a raw material or finished goods warehouse (either yours or that of a supplier or customer), do you look at and ask questions about the amount of obsolete and excess (O&E) stock that exists, how often the stock is turned over, the level of traceability, the age of the stock, what volume and value of raw materials or finished goods is kept and why, and whether FIFO can be demonstrated and bypassed? For senior managers, the answers to these questions can reveal a lot about the policies and culture of an organization.

Supplier Development

It is in our interest to help our suppliers and raise their quality levels. A lot of time and expense is spent in getting a new supplier set up, and changing suppliers is not something to be undertaken lightly; we should be as thorough in taking on a new supplier as we are in taking on a senior manager. It can be money well spent to send in representatives from the Quality and Engineering departments to carry out an audit, particularly when dealing with smaller suppliers that might not have the technical expertise or resources that we would prefer.

We should send our own people into suppliers to help develop relationships with key personnel. Also, we should invite suppliers to our line to see how their product is used. If we can't do this, can we perhaps send them a finished product that they can analyze or send them a video of their product in use?

It can be beneficial to ask our suppliers to meet our employees, who can usually explain clearly any issues they are having with the supplier's product. If we cannot get the supplier on site, is it practical to bring one or two of our employees to the supplier site? Of course, this may not be possible if the supplier is far away, but a video conference might help.

Suppliers usually want to embed themselves with their customers (as we want to do with *our* customers), so we should enter into agreements with suppliers with this in mind. We want to ensure both organizations have this type of relationship.

CHAPTER SUMMARY

In this chapter, we reviewed details of what might be included in a supplier contract, and we looked at supplier selection. We also reviewed specific aspects of purchasing, receiving, inspection, storage, and supplier development.

Questions

1. What are your supplier selection criteria? Are they communicated to the relevant personnel?

2. Do you consider the impact of supplier selection on other departments? Is there a formal process for departments to input their requirements and appeal a decision?

3. How would you regard the quality and thoroughness of your supplier contracts?

4. How do you control stock and traceability?

CHAPTER ELEVEN

* * *

Quality and
Change Management

CHAPTER OUTLINE:

In this chapter we take a fresh look at change and why it often does not go smoothly. By understanding why this happens, we can rethink our approach in order to produce a better outcome. We then briefly look at some change techniques.

Much has been written, and continues to be written, on change management. In this chapter, I focus on some core issues that can help change to happen effectively.

Some research indicates that it can be better to let people know what they will lose by not changing, rather than trying to emphasize the benefits. Let's be realistic here and acknowledge that often there are few, if any, benefits for the ordinary employee in going with a change (if there were an obvious benefit to the employee, then change would be relatively easy). What I mean is that changes are usually where we as managers are trying to improve productivity, profitability, or quality, and these changes don't always improve the lot of the employee. We say to employees that the changes will improve our service to the customer or improve the ability of the organization to compete in the market, but employees are often reluctant to change how things are done. They see it as just another cost-saving exercise, with the ordinary employee bearing the brunt of the impact. For most employees, there is such a disconnect between what they do and what the organization is trying to do that they can't or don't relate to the reasons put forward by management. The perception is often that the organization is trying to squeeze more out of them with nothing in return (and possibly the threat of layoffs mentioned). It should therefore be no surprise that they don't seem to respond to our reasoning or logic. Employees don't see the management accounts on a weekly basis to see the worsening financial position of the organization, they don't see the threat of a new product or new competitor, they don't see the impact of new regulations. Why don't we explain things better to employees? Regular communication is key. Does your organization hold periodic meetings with staff? Do you present a summary of the opportunities and threats to the organization?

People need to be ready to change. We need to set the scene and prepare them. This can include showing the dangers of doing nothing and the downside of the current situation. We also need to understand people's fear of the unknown and try to make the unknown, known. This will reduce the barriers to change.

As mentioned in a previous chapter, we didn't reach our own decision on what needs to be done overnight, so why should we expect our employees to be any different? We might have been analyzing data for weeks or months before deciding on the savings or changes that are needed. What is the risk in letting our employees see this data? It's not necessary to provide exact financial data; it might be enough to show the trend or graphs in percentages).

We need to bring employees on a similar journey to our own, from where things are to where we need to be, and to emphasize the milestones along the way. By milestones, I mean the key internal and external forces and timescales that are operating on our organization. If we do this in a genuine way, and are seen to be planning the changes and doing the analysis with them, not to them, there will be a much better chance of the change being accepted. It needs to be a continual communication process, not a one-time staff meeting where management announce various significant changes. Can we present the information at intervals that show what is happening and that the decision the organization is making is the best long-term solution for the business? By repeating the message at intervals, we allow time for the change to percolate through the organization; by the time of the actual change, it is no longer seen as a big deal. Of course, there will be times when the best long-term solution for the business may mean letting people go, shutting facilities, or reducing benefits. Nobody is going to say they are OK with that, whether they are directly affected or not, or no matter how long they have been aware of such a possibility.

How can quality and quality personnel help in the changing environment in which we work?

- Quality personnel usually have to deal with many different departments and thus gain an oversight into how an organization is put together. This can help in anticipating potential roadblocks to change.

- Quality personnel are often engaged in the art of persuasion, to convince production or purchasing or logistics or finance or IT why something has to be changed or stopped or rechecked. Persuasion is a key change management skill.

- Quality personnel have a range of tools they use for problem solving or continual improvement. Change can be thought of as both problem solving and continual improvement.

- Improving quality (in the broadest sense of the word) can mean improving our competitive position.

It can be argued that in capitalism, we are all just a number no matter what our level is in an organization. Everyone has to perform or be shunted out. In fact, even that is not enough. You could be a top performer but working in the wrong department at the wrong time when cuts are being made. If this is your view, it's easy to see why people don't jump on the change bandwagon with enthusiasm. People are afraid of the impact of the change on them.

A further issue is that many ordinary employees do not get job satisfaction in their work, it is just a means to an end. As a result they don't feel a great affinity to the organization. As we hear more and more of portfolio careers, it is easy to see why people are less committed to any one employer. On top of that, many people have been burnt with previous layoffs, or seen their friends affected by it.

So planning for change is crucial for any organization, and some useful tools and techniques include these:

- Use force-field analysis to look at the driving and resisting forces in relation to the change.

- Use the Socratic method; pose the questions and issues currently requiring change and let people come up with possible answers, thus taking at least some ownership of the change.

- Look at job enlargement. Can people do more of the processes that make a complete part or provide a complete service? Job enlargement can help the customer as well as the employee; customers usually prefer to deal with just one person, rather than be passed around through various departments. But we need to be careful not to just end up giving a person more work.

- Look at job enrichment. Can we give employees more authority and responsibility? (Remember our discussion on authority, mastery, and purpose—AMP.) The same caveat applies here as in the previous point.

- Promote, publicly recognize and reward, or give extra money to those who are behaving in the desired manner.

- Try to involve those affected by the change.

- Decide who are the critical people to get on-side. Who are the natural leaders?

- Consider reciprocity. If we want them to do something for the organization, what can we do to help *them*? What are *their* issues and frustrations with the job?

- Explain the challenges facing the organization/department/ industry, and what will happen if nothing changes.

- Explain the challenges being faced by the organization and ask employees to come up with possible solutions (with rewards for any solutions subsequently implemented).

- Can we propose more than one option? There may be more than one way of getting to our objective, so that people feel they have some control over what gets implemented.

- Run a pilot/trial.

- Look for the low-hanging fruit, the easy savings.

- Is there visible top management support for the new behavior?

- People often need to be unhappy with their current situation before they want to change. Even then, there is no guarantee. How many people eat badly, or smoke, or drink excessively, knowing it's bad for them and wishing they could change their habits? Are people dissatisfied with their current situation? If so, they will be more ready for change.

- Look at the Kurt Lewin model of Unfreeze-Change-Refreeze: unfreezing the old behavior, introducing the new way of doing things, and then refreezing the new behavior (i.e., reinforcing or rewarding the new ways of doing things).

- Let people have their say.

- Go behind the drama to get to the facts.

- Get the reasons behind people's views. Why do they hold them?

- Emphasize the similarities between the old way and the new way.

- Remember, improvement my mean stopping or eliminating something you are currently doing.

- Focus on future solutions.

- Look for early success.

- Change the reward systems.

- Practice the principle of equifinality; let people come up with the "how" themselves, as long as the desired end result is achieved.

- Start a conversation with the seed of the change required; for example, say, "Our main customer has said they will only deal with organizations that have ISO 9001 certification." This sets the scene.

CHAPTER SUMMARY

In this chapter, we took a look at why change might not go smoothly and looked at some of the reasons for this. Change is a journey and we, as senior managers, must bring our employees along on that journey rather than just presenting a *fait accompli* and expecting everything to go OK. We finished up by looking briefly at some of the more common change techniques.

Questions

1. How well do you set the scene for change? Do you explain the downsides of the current situation, as well as the benefits of the new situation?

2. Do you allow time for the change to percolate through the organization, so that by the time it is officially announced, it is almost no longer news?

3. Are there any ways of increasing job satisfaction for employees as a result of the change?

4. Do you look at the different ways of communicating change to see which is best?

5. Do you look at available change tools to determine which might apply in your specific instance?

CHAPTER TWELVE

*** *** ***

Quality and Training

CHAPTER OUTLINE:

In this chapter, we look at what might be included as part of every employee's training. We revisit why we should invest in our people, what types of training work best, and different ways of verifying that training has been carried out and is understood.

A key role for QA should be training. All employees should know not just how to do their own job, but also some of the following, where appropriate:

- How to describe their own processes in flowchart form
- The concept of Supplier-Input-Process-Output-Customer (SIPOC) and the internal customer
- How to audit, and tips on auditing
- Root cause analysis techniques
- Problem solving techniques
- The philosophy of continual improvement
- The concept of inspecting one's own work, and how this can be done in an unbiased manner
- Statistical Process Control (SPC)
- Visual controls
- Mistake proofing
- 8D problem solving
- Pareto analysis and histograms
- The 5 whys approach to root cause identification

- The 5S approach to good housekeeping and things being in the correct place

- Basic quality tools including Pareto, fishbone, FMEA, risk management

People should to be encouraged to produce a flow chart of what they do and to make suggestions for improvement. Flow charts should show the paperwork involved (instructions and records), the checks to be done, who is responsible, any non value-added activity, the records involved, and inputs and outputs, particularly at the start and end of their process.

We should empower employees to suggest (and implement) improvements as long as they meet certain criteria (e.g., records and checks completed).

Everyone should be trained in auditing. People should audit their internal suppliers and internal customers (or audit a different area from where they're working), and encourage positive suggestions. This can help generate cross-fertilization of ideas and improvements, as long as the groundwork is done to stop people reacting negatively to suggestions from their internal customers.

Most training fails because people are not able to apply it afterwards, or they try something new and fail. We need to ensure the work environment is ready for new ideas. Do we have a culture of learning? Remember studies indicate that if the training happens too long before it can be applied, it will not be successful.

How do we ensure in our organization that training is effective and that what has been learned is implemented? In most cases, we verify the effectiveness of training by looking at someone's performance before and after training, or look at what someone could not do before training but can now do. More thought should be placed on what is done before training is undertaken. For example, is there a small form for potential trainees to complete to indicate why they are doing the training, what they hope to get from it, and what they expect to be able to do differently or better as a result of the training? This makes it easier to ensure the training was worthwhile.

Why is on-the-job training seen as the most useful and what can we learn from it? Because it's relevant, it's at the place of work, the trainer is usually an expert, the trainee gets the chance to try it out there and then, and there is someone there to help correct mistakes (i.e., there is good feedback on trying out what has been learned). We could build on this by encouraging our internal experts (which could be all of our managers, but it could be any level of employee) to draw up presentations or short courses on their area of expertise. This will then supplement the on-the-job training, and give the organization at least a basic and documented understanding of what is involved in that process.

It is useful to have a list of documents/procedures/courses that are relevant to each role that a person undertakes when they join an organization. When these are complete, each one should be signed off by the trainer and employee, and dated. These records should show the revision number of the document/procedure/course taken, to ensure that people have been trained to the latest revision. As part of ongoing key document changes, the relevant employees can sign off (electronically or on paper) to show that they have reviewed the latest document revision. This is especially important in regulated industries.

A few comments about online training. There are plenty of free and cheap courses available, and some are very good. Why do organizations not make more use of these? Organizations should allow employees a certain number of hours per month for online training. If people are able to use Excel better, or learn about finance, or understand motivation or marketing, and they can do this for free or for a nominal amount, why would we not encourage this? The organization will benefit immediately.

Some people question why we should train people if there is a chance they will leave. There are several answers to this. One answer is that people need to be trained to do their job properly, effectively, efficiently, and in a manner that suits the individual organization. If there is no standardization in how things are done, then inefficiencies must result. It can also be argued that by investing in people through training, we will actually encourage them to stay. Good training will improve how the organization operates and should transfer new skills, ideas, and techniques into the organization. These ideas and techniques will then remain in the organization even if the original person leaves.

> *"If you think training is expensive, try ignorance."*
> – Peter Drucker

If we want the best out of people, we need to invest in them. And we undermine that philosophy when people are let go, departments are closed down, wages are reduced, shorter hours are introduced, and benefits are reduced. Of course these things happen in the open marketplace where most organizations operate. The point here is that whether you agree or not that people are our greatest asset, they are certainly our most flexible asset and should be viewed accordingly.

For example, maybe we should look at whether employees are willing to be trained in a different area, so they can stay with the organization, rather than face a layoff. From the organization's point of view, it is usually cheaper to transfer an employee (with satisfactory performance) than to recruit a new person.

Procedures, whether in text or flowchart or pictorial form, should be mainly used for training purposes. We should have key documents of no more than one page (or one screen) at each station or process (or part of a process). How often will someone turn a page or call up a second screen several times a day, on a daily basis? It's not going to happen. But we try to force employees to do this by making them press something or scan something before they can move to the next part of the process. This is only reinforcing the message that we don't trust our employees. In some organizations we compound the cost by date-stamping the instructions, such that they must be re-printed every week or every day.

The better solution is to train employees with the full procedure or work instruction and then rely on the one-page reminder sheet. It will greatly reduce paperwork on the line. If a process changes such that the procedure or work instruction needs to be changed, then we bring all affected employees through the training again. Our training records should say that the person was trained on the process and also indicate what revision of the procedure/work instruction was used. Other circumstances call for training: a new hire, an employee transfer, or an employee who has not worked on a process for a certain period of time. Technology is becoming more and more useful from a training viewpoint through the use of augmented reality.

We wouldn't be happy if bus drivers or accountants had to check a manual every day before performing the next step of their work. There's no law that says we *must* have the document on the line—it just needs to be available. We should look at mistake-proofing the job and providing proper training. The design of the work should lead people to do the job right, and it should flag up immediately if something is done wrong.

I am not arguing against the use of a checklist *where it benefits the work;* it can be used to require an employee to tick a box or sign a checklist to verify all the steps have been actioned. The downside of this is that it can become a tick box exercise, where people tick all the boxes at the end of a job or shift or before the job is even started. It's important to be flexible. What is the best way for *our* organization to ensure the job is done correctly?

It is appropriate that records are kept of actions performed, when, and by whom; that makes sense. But we need to have confidence in our training and in our staff. We need to train them well, maybe have a yearly refresher on the key procedures or instructions, and keep a training log.

How do we ensure that work instructions or procedures and their updates are highlighted to relevant people and that they are read and understood by those people? Some options are:

- Use different color sheets for one week after issuing.

- Have a popup on a screen.

- Send automated emails to ensure that people read the document and "sign" that this has been done.

- Send a sheet around that people have to sign, to show they have read and understood the new document or new revision.

- For every new or updated document, include a few questions that people have to answer. These questions should focus on the changes to a document where a revision change occurs. Then at least you have some record of people understanding the changes.

CHAPTER SUMMARY

In this chapter we looked at why we should invest in training our employees. We showed areas in which everyone should be trained, and we looked at what makes training more effective.

Questions

1. What common training is done in your organization?

2. Do you review the effectiveness of training by checking whether anything changes as a result of the training?

3. How do you ensure people are trained to the latest documents?

4. Does your organization conduct exit interviews? If so, what happens to that information?

CHAPTER THIRTEEN

✳ ✳ ✳

Quality Management Systems (QMS)

CHAPTER OUTLINE:

In this chapter, we review elements and components of a QMS, we ask whether a QMS is only "consistent repetition," we look at the quality manual, we discuss integrated management systems (IMS), and we ask why we need certification and how useful it is.

When we talk about quality management systems (QMS), we are usually referring to the international standard ISO 9001. In order to get the best out of a QMS, we need to look at not just the *content*, but also the *intent* of the standard.

ISO 9001 has been described a system that encourages "consistent repetition," which is OK as far as it goes and has benefits, but we should be looking for a lot more than this. We can find more in the standard if we dig a little further and look for the areas of continual improvement. We can also look at ISO 9004 for inspiration.

We know that the focus in the standard is on the process but we should not forget how these processes affect the financial performance of the organization.

The processes should drive the QMS, not the other way round. Fundamentally, we need to use ISO 9001 as a tool. We should have our own documented processes, records, and procedures and then look at how far this complies with the requirements of the standard. We should not start with the standard and write our procedures around it. If we do this, we will derive minimal benefit from certification.

ISO certification gives you confidence that:

- There is a system
- There is document/record control
- There is a system for non-conformances
- The processes are auditable

The increase in second-party audits (where an organization audits its suppliers) is an indication of the decline in confidence in ISO certification. But is this a problem with the standard, or have people assumed too much of the ISO certification? ISO 9001 tries to cover every base in terms of being applicable to any organization, and this results in it being very generic. That is not a criticism of the standard, just how it has to be. Where industries have felt it is insufficient, they have added their own requirements (e.g., automotive, medical, and telecommunications).

We should ask ourselves why we are ISO 9001 certified or why we are going for certification. Is it a customer requirement, is it just something that everyone else seems to be doing so we don't want to be left out? Do we need certification to be able to get government or private contracts? These reasons are externally driven.

They may all be valid reasons. If a major customer says we need to be certified, then that is a good reason to consider certification. But we may not be fully committed to the thrust and intent of the standard if we feel it is something we *must* do. We may end up just going through the motions and doing the bare minimum to achieve it. This is one reason why many larger organizations still conduct their own audits of suppliers. Having the certification does not mean everyone can turn off and do nothing on the QMS until the next annual audit, when there is a panic to get things in place.

Also, using ISO 9001 accreditation as part of your supplier selection criteria could be viewed as a lazy way out if it is the only selection criteria and if it is not followed up with more rigorous investigation.

I believe we can only get the best out of ISO 9001 if there are at least some internal reasons for certification. Internal reasons might be:

- We want to document what we're doing.

- We want to be consistent in what we're doing.

- We are losing knowledge when people leave.

- We want to get feedback on how our QMS is performing (all organizations have a QMS, whether documented or not and whether certified or not. We all need to know whether something is good or not, or how to measure something, or if we are dealing with a reliable supplier).

- People don't know what to do when something unusual happens (this can equally apply to manufacturing or service or to a finance department).

- We want to be able to demonstrate that our products are designed and tested appropriately to ensure they perform safely and fulfil customer or market requirements.

- We want to measure how we're doing and continually improve.

These are some of the potential benefits of certification to ISO 9001. Let's assume we have successfully scaled that hurdle and we want to go ahead with certification.

When going for ISO 9001, a good place to start is to get people to document what they are *actually* doing; then review these documents under the ISO 9001 criteria. As part of this process documentation exercise, it is useful for people to note the critical to quality (CTQ) areas in their processes and then look at how we can make the process robust for these items. By robust, I mean things like:

- Designing the work system so that a job cannot be completed incorrectly; at least it will be obvious immediately if something is wrong.

- Having an inline inspection step to detect errors. For example, we could put parts made at workstation 1 into a jig at workstation 2 to automatically detect any discrepancy (i.e., parts will not fit into the jig). Or we could have a process where the first job of any employee was to verify the work done by the previous employee (and/or where the last job of any employee is to make sure what they have processed has been done correctly). This could mean checking every item or transaction or taking a sample from the start, middle, and end; with computer or online tasks, we should be able to automate this, and in fact let the first operator know immediately if something has not been completed.

- Having a high process capability such that if parts go slightly outside the nominal value, they will still be within the specification. For example, if we have to make parts with a tolerance of +/-0.5mm, we could use equipment with a much higher capability index and set our control limits at +/-0.1mm. This would help us detect problems before the parts went out of specification, thus preventing scrap.

- Having a good alert system that will show a non-conformance as soon as possible and as early in the process as possible. For example, if we are filling out an online form and we leave any mandatory field blank, the system will not allow us to progress to the next stage.

Where possible, we should train people so that they can draw up or at least contribute to their own process flow chart/procedure. This might be the individual employee, a team, or a department manager. The Quality department should be supporting other departments in creating procedures, rather than create the actual procedure. Involving QA can also help ensure that the same format is used throughout the organization.

The next level down from a procedure is forms. When we create forms, we need to ask questions about the function of such forms. Is the information logged anywhere else? Why do we want that information? What do we do with that information? Ideally, we need to do more than just file it away (we may need to keep it for regulatory purposes, but this should not stop us trying to get useful information out of it first). Can we incorporate the information required onto an existing form or document that the person is already filling out (soft or hard copy)? Does it make any difference if there is a record or not?

Our thought process should be this: what is the minimum amount of paperwork or electronic documentation we need in order to provide evidence and confidence that the job has been done correctly and meets any regulatory requirement?

Instead of having lengthy text procedures, why not aim for a flow chart procedure? I show a version of such a procedure flowchart in Appendix 4. It won't suit every situation, but it should help reduce the number of pages. The other advantage of doing this exercise is that it helps us focus on the key elements of any process and highlights any non-value-adding activities that are taking place.

The top-level document in organizations that have ISO 9001 certification is the quality manual (no longer a mandatory document in ISO 9001:2015). The quality manual has become an almost redundant document, from a quality viewpoint, but it can still play a role in showing how everything hangs together in a QMS. The manual has sometimes been used as a marketing tool, where we give a copy to our customers or potential customers. The reason we can do this is because it usually contains no sensitive information. The quality manual only states that we comply with the requirements of the standard—it doesn't have to state how we do this, and many quality manuals merely refer to specific procedures or instructions. Some organizations have a 5- or 10-page quality manual; others have gone a step further and have a one- or two-page quality manual. If an organization still wishes to have a quality manual, there is a good argument to have only one page per clause (or sub-clause) in the standard. If we need more than one page, then I would suggest we are putting information into our quality manual that really belongs in our procedures manual.

An integrated management system (which usually involves all or a combination of ISO 9001 – quality, ISO 14001 – environment, and ISO 45001/OHSAS 18001 – health and safety) is likely to require the following in order to become part of the quality professional's knowledge base:

- Corporate governance
- Corporate social responsibility
- Awareness of regulatory requirements for environment, and health and safety

- Enterprise risk assessment, management, and monitoring:
  - Organization risks
  - Quality risks
  - Environmental aspects
  - Occupational health and safety risks
  - Information security
  - Relevant sector requirements
- Integrated procurement requirements

A list of ISO management system standards can be found at: http://www.iso.org/iso/mss-list.

There are also various guide documents from ISO on other areas such as energy (ISO 50001), CSR (ISO 26000), risk management (ISO 31000), quality plans (ISO 10005), people involvement (ISO 10018), realizing financial benefits (ISO 10014), project management (ISO 21500), configuration management (ISO 10007), quality management in projects (ISO 10006), training (ISO 10015), business continuity (ISO 22301), and several more. If you go to the ISO website (www.iso.org) and key in numbers between 10002 and 10019 in the search box, you will see guides for various areas. It is a pity that these are not advertised more, because they are good guides. (Guides are not auditable by a certification body.)

ISO has released what is called "Annex SL." This is a document that gives the high-level layout for the main certifiable standards such as ISO 9001, ISO 14001, and others. For these standards, they will all share the following sections:

Introduction

1. Scope
2. Normative references
3. Terms and definitions
4. Context of the organization
5. Leadership
6. Planning
7. Support
8. Operation
9. Performance evaluation
10. Improvement

With the introduction of this standardized layout, organizations will not need to keep changing their documentation titles or numbering. Of course, organizations never needed to do this, but many did for the benefit of making it easier to link to the standard. The other benefit of annex SL is that for companies using multiple standards, it makes the Integrated Management Standards approach more consistent.

Figure 14 illustrates an overall view of a quality management system (QMS).

From the requirements of the standard, we work our way down through our documentation until we produce evidence that we have done what we said we are doing (in our procedures and work instructions).

Our documentation structure should suit our organization; our procedures should be based on processes or departments, rather than ISO clauses. This is fine if the procedures address the clauses in the standard. The Quality department can verify this.

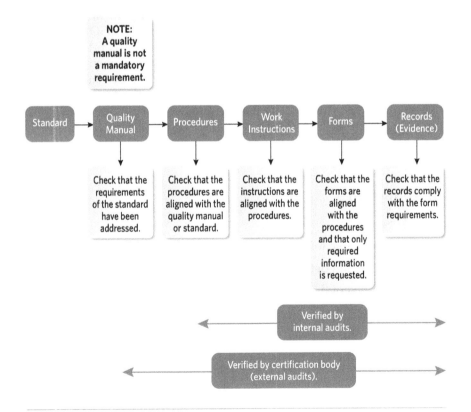

Figure 14 A quality management system (QMS).

Getting ISO 9001 certification should not be the goal of the Quality department or an organization. The goal should be a commitment to improve the organization, using the tools and criteria in the standard.

Have we, as senior managers, even read any of the organization's procedures or ISO 9001, or gone to an executive introduction to ISO 9001? Do we think that this is something only the Quality department should consider? Why not pick a procedure and see whether it makes sense to us, and then go to that area and see whether it is being put into practice? This can be part of the auditing procedure, which I cover in the next chapter.

Many questions have been raised over the years regarding certification bodies (CBs):

- How competent are the CB auditors; do they have or need experience in the organization's business or service they are auditing?

- What do you do if you disagree with a CB auditor? Is it worth the risk of making them defensive, and possibly ending up with a worse result?

- What should you do if your auditor is too easy?

- How do we resolve the inherent problem of both paying a CB and asking them to be our impartial examiner?

It is certainly preferable for an auditor to have some knowledge or experience in your industry; otherwise it's possible for an auditor to miss important elements that need special attention; it's also possible for the audited organization to steer an auditor away from certain areas that they want to avoid.

It is important to stick to the standard. For example, if an auditor highlights an issue, it is fair to ask where that issue is addressed in the standard. If the auditor cannot back up his statements, you are entitled to feel suspicious. In any event, a good auditor will not become defensive. A good auditor will either point to the relevant clause in the standard and explain why a certain item needs to be in place, or admit the mistake and correct the request.

The organization must decide for itself how it wishes to proceed. It is certainly reasonable for an organization to request a different auditor for future audits, and this might be the most practical response to this situation.

As to the problem of both paying a CB and asking them to be an impartial examiner? I'm not convinced anyone has squared that circle yet.

These are questions you should ask before you select a certification body for your ISO 9001 accreditation.

Remember that all ISO management system standards and guidelines undergo periodic update; just because your systems are OK at present, there is no guarantee that they will meet the requirements of the next revision of the standard or guideline.

One comment about software used to manage quality. We must push for one system to handle all aspects of a QMS. There is a lot to be said for choosing an off-the-shelf, all-in-one system. If we choose to develop a system in-house, it should be a simple system that can be extended easily using, for example, an SQL database.

As regards paper versus electronic records, ISO 9001 already allows soft versions of documents and records. With proper electronic records, retrieval is easy, records do not deteriorate, there are no external storage costs involved, and anyone can access the records; paper documents and records should only be kept where there is a statutory, industry, or contractual requirement to do so. Even if forms are completed on paper, we can see whether we can digitize these documents afterwards.

Mike Micklewright has published an excellent book on ISO, *Lean ISO 9001*.

CHAPTER SUMMARY

In this chapter we reviewed the key elements of a QMS and we looked at content versus the intent of the standard. We looked at IMS, and we finished by asking ourselves why we get certified and what benefit it brings to the organization.

Questions

1. Why are you certified to ISO 9001?

2. Does your QMS benefit your organization? How?

3. Have you read any of the procedures relevant to your area of responsibility?

4. Are you happy with your certification body, the body that conducts the ISO audits on your organization? Have you ever met with them, to get a feel for what they think about your organization's QMS and its approach to quality?

CHAPTER FOURTEEN

* * *

Auditing

CHAPTER OUTLINE:

In this chapter, we look at the role of audits, how we can structure them better to get more out of them, and how we might conduct audits, including core questions that are applicable to any audit.

Auditing has received a bad name from various sources over the years (usually by those who are due to be or have been audited!). This is due to a fundamental misunderstanding of what auditing is about. Auditing is not meant to catch people or to try to find mistakes. Auditing is meant to demonstrate that the system is working as it should be, but it is important to remember that an audit reflects only a snapshot at one moment in time.

This can also be a reason why having quality personnel do audits may not be a good idea. The Quality department is still often seen as a "policeman," checking up on others; to add the audit function only reinforces this image.

Audits can, if planned and conducted properly, help improve how systems operate, and this is where our focus should be. Ultimately, if audits are fulfilling their improvement objective, then we can focus on what happens between audits and not on what happens *during* audits.

An auditor interviews, observes, reviews documents, examines records, logs all documents viewed and people interviewed, and reviews the results of previous internal and external audits. It's important to remember that auditing is done against certain criteria or requirements—ISO 9001 or internal procedures or instructions. There must always be something to audit against.

Everything should be kept fact-based. An auditor needs to be able to refer to a specific requirement, particularly if a non-conformance is being raised.

When doing quality audits, it is normal to choose a process and audit examples from this process; we then compare the actual situation with the procedure or work instruction. While doing this, records are kept of the names of those involved (this links to training and record control), what, if any, equipment is used (this links to calibration and record control), what components are used (this links to purchasing, incoming inspection, stock rotation, and record control), what controlled documents are used (this links to documented information and revision numbers). In doing one process, we are checking various clauses of the standard. This is the process approach (the old approach was clause-based).

We should audit not only for the purpose of conforming to the requirements of ISO 9001. We should also think about what we want to gain from audits, so we should feel free to add other questions or areas that are relevant to our organization.

Should you use a checklist? Checklists are good for inexperienced auditors, but they can be limiting. There can be a tendency to feel that a good audit has been conducted just because all the sections are filled in. Checklists certainly have their uses, but we need to use them intelligently; we need to know why we are using them and consider the associated pitfalls. Using checklists might demonstrate conformance, but used on their own, they rarely generate improvement. Auditors need to be able to ask (relevant) questions outside of the checklist, when something unusual comes up or a comment is made by an auditee, or certain records cannot be located, or a change is not documented.

Who Should Conduct Audits?

In my view, there is a definite role for what are called layered audits, where people from different levels of the organization conduct or assist with audits. The audits might be less detailed as one goes higher up the organization, but they give a fresh perspective on a process or department because different people are looking at it. I would further argue that this requirement should be built into the objectives and KPIs of every manager and/or director. Even if the senior manager is simply accompanying the auditor, this is still beneficial; it shows that management are interested in what is happening at lower levels and that Quality is regarded as important.

When devising an audit plan and schedule, we should consider the importance of the areas being audited, and perhaps give a weighting to certain areas. We may wish to audit certain areas more than once per year, areas that are critical to our organization.

After an audit has been completed and the results written up, what then happens to that information? Whom does it go to, what do they do with it, what action is taken? Without completing the loop, the value of the audit is lost.

The QMS is not the documented system; the QMS is the process used to produce the product or service, and it is this process that we should be auditing.

Have you ever looked at audit results to see what is being found? You might be interested in an audit of your Finance or Purchasing or R&D department.

General Auditing Tips and Requirements

- Audits are fact-finding missions; it is vital that you stick to facts and actual documents and records.

- Audits are not fault-finding missions; you are not trying to find things wrong, you are trying to confirm that things are right.

- Think of audits like a balance sheet—requirements on one hand, and evidence on the other.

- Remember, a document can be a procedure, record, form, template, drawing, or report and it can be electronic or on paper.

- Before doing an audit, it is important that you have a copy of the procedure and read through it, plus any associated documents, forms, specifications, and so on. Highlight any section that refers to a record or other controlled document so that you can check for these items during the audit.

- For an audit trail to be acceptable, you must log the document details you looked at (document name, date, revision, anyone who approved or reviewed the document, and in some cases who created it; training record, calibration record, purchase order number viewed, and drawing number).

- Before doing an audit, have a look at the results of previous audits, both internal and external, and verify that any non-conformances have been effectively addressed.

- Keep the language as neutral and unbiased as possible; rather than saying "The technician didn't fill out the test reports correctly" it's much better to say "There is no evidence that test reports have been completed in accordance with documented procedures."

- Look at the status and importance of each process or section being audited. Status can be defined as how a particular department, discipline, facility, or process is performing against established policies, goals, objectives, and expectations.

Some questions to ask would be:

- What are the performance indicators for this process, area, group, or department?
- What does the performance history indicate?
- Have there been changes in process, equipment, personnel, or management?
- Has the area or department been restructured or reorganized?

• Try to do the audit as a process, rather than just one procedure at a time.

• When auditing, simple open questions are usually the best. So, for example:

- "Tell me briefly what you do and what you are trying to achieve." Listen for handover points or records kept. Ask if what they do is as per the procedure or work instruction. If not, why not?

- "How do you know what to do?" Look at training and/or knowledge of the applicable procedure or work instruction. Workers need not have the procedure in front of them or on their PC, but they should know where to find it (ask them to find it) and they should have a broad idea of what it contains.

- "How do you know whether something is done correctly?" Here we are not only checking knowledge of the procedure but also knowledge of the criteria applicable to what they are doing (e.g., adherence to a schedule or drawing or tender, due date for invoicing or paying a supplier, out of date training certificates, specification, KPI). Ask about the KPI history. How has it changed over the last few months or years, how are the records kept, what actions are taken based on the results, and are there any recurring issues?

- "What do you do if something is not right?" Workers should have knowledge of the procedure; if something goes wrong who do they tell? How do they identify the non-conforming item or document so that someone else could pick it up and process it?

- "Would you say you are meeting your objectives?" Sometimes individuals are not clear on their objectives and this question can often be met with silence.

- "What records do you keep?"

- "Have there been any improvements made to this process in the last 12 months?" If yes, note them as positives.

- "Why are you doing it this way? Could it be done better (quicker, simpler, less double handling or copying)?" These can be noted as observations or opportunities for improvement.
- "Who are your suppliers?" This refers to the internal or external suppliers.
- "What are the process inputs?" These can be documents, drawings, materials, instructions, or information.
- "What are the process outputs?" These can be documents, drawings, materials, instructions, or information.
- "Who are your customers?" This can mean internal or external customers.

- Before finishing your audit, review your findings with the auditee, and get agreement on what was found during the audit, preferably getting a signature on the audit sheet.
- Remember to record positives and to mention these to the auditee.
- Ultimately, we are trying to show:
  - What is being done is what was planned.
  - That the system meets the requirements of the procedure or standard.
  - That the system is meeting the organization's objectives.
  - That it is effectively implemented.
  - That due regard is given to criticality and, where the system is not meeting requirements, corrective actions are recommended.

Finally, we need to feed the results of this audit (internal, customer, certification body) into the next set of internal audits so that we can be sure that those items raised have been addressed.

All of the points above could be looked at in terms of how to do a good conformance-type audit. There is much talk about value-added audits, where we do more than just confirm that things are as they should be. In these audits, we encourage open questions and allow suggestions from the auditor and auditee. These can be a good source of improvement, but the danger is that they become too open and ideas get logged that should not be. Because they are now recorded in the audit, some follow-up is required. This is not to say they should not be tried; just be aware of possible pitfalls that might clog up the system.

It should be noted that there is nothing in ISO 9001 to stop people doing value-added audits, as long as they conform to the requirements in the standard.

CHAPTER SUMMARY

In this chapter, we looked at internal audits, why we do them, how to get more out of them, who should do them, what important questions any auditor should ask. We listed some important auditing tips and introduced concepts such as layered audits and value-added audits.

Questions

1. Has senior management ever looked at the results of internal or external audits?

2. Has senior management ever conducted, participated in, or accompanied an auditor during an audit? Why not try it?

3. What benefit are you getting from internal or external audits? Is demonstrating conformance sufficient? (It might be.)

4. Do you encourage value-added audits?

5. Do you encourage more than just the quality department to get involved in conducting audits? Is it part of every manager's KPI?

CHAPTER FIFTEEN

* * *

Quality and
Lean Management

CHAPTER OUTLINE:
In this chapter, we outline some of the key elements of lean, we briefly discuss the concepts of value-add versus non value-add, and we introduce the philosophy of Theory of Constraints.

Lean can mean many things to many people. It involves concepts such as these:

- Kanban (using a "pull" system rather than a "push" system).

- Kaizen (a term for continual improvement).

- 5S (a process for organizing, streamlining, and tidying the workplace).

- 1-piece flow.

- Theory of constraints (TOC), focusing on throughput and bottlenecks/constraints.

- SMED (single minute exchange of dies).

- Visual factory: self-ordering, self-explaining, self-regulating, and self-improving. In a visual workplace, floors don't exist simply to walk on or hold things up. They show us where it is safe to walk, where good and bad materials are located, and where we are supposed to work. Benches are not merely surfaces on which to place parts, documents, and tools; they indicate the exact location of the tools, documents, and equipment we use and show us when things are missing.

- No waste: a common approach is to categorize waste into TIMWOOD PM acronym—Transport, Inventory, Movement, Waiting, Over-processing, Over-production, Defects. Some people add under-utilised People, and Material under-utilization.

- Just in Time.
- Mistake proofing.
- Value stream mapping (VSM)—value added, non value added, non value added but essential.
- Reduced lead time.
- Reduced stock.
- Reduced WIP.
- Total productive maintenance.
- Takt time.
- Line balancing.
- OEE.
- Standard work.
- Cells.
- Outsourcing.
- Machine losses: equipment breakdown, changeovers, short stops, idling, start-up rejects, production rejects, short runs.
- Flow and pull. Flow of material, information, documentation.

Lean management is system based, and focuses on reducing waste and non-value-adding activities. Many books and articles have been written about lean and how to implement it. It is not the purpose of this book to go into the detail of lean; what is included here is just a snapshot of some of the key issues.

Implementing lean often starts with the 5S approach, followed by value stream mapping (VSM).

VSM starts with inventory and involves everyone in identifying the main wastes and bottlenecks. It can be complicated to set up and conduct VSM and it takes time for a complete process, but it does show up clearly the amount of non-value added time time "wasted." A simplified version of VSM might be appropriate for a department or individual process or a small organization.

A spaghetti diagram is a tool that can reveal the movement of employees or materials between workstations. The aim is to remove the unnecessary movement of people, documents, or materials.

Inspection is non value adding, so it is reasonable to ask where we are doing it, how often we are doing it, and why we are doing it. Are we inspecting because we don't trust our suppliers? If so, then we need to review our suppliers, why we are using them, and what actions can be implemented by the suppliers to improve their consistency. Are we inspecting because we don't trust the process? If so, then the obvious next step is to investigate that process and adjust it until it is capable. Are we inspecting because we don't trust our people? If so, then we need a culture shift and training to change this. Organizations today cannot afford to have people whose sole job is to inspect the work of others. We either train our employees or we redesign our processes so that non-conformances are prevented or detected as early as possible in the process.

The amount of work in progress (WIP) is a measure of the amount of inefficiency in an organization. You do not need to be a brain surgeon to know something is not right when you see a stack of components at a machine or a stack of documents at a workstation. The next step is to ask "why?" and then when ask "why?" again. This is often referred to as the "5-whys" process, where you keep asking "why" until the root cause of the problem is found. Note that it may require fewer or more than five whys to reach the root cause.

Reducing inventory is the last thing to do; it's important to remove the other problems first (bad quality, machine downtime, and inefficient processes) and have good flow and reliable suppliers before taking out the safety net that is raw material or WIP stock. Do not remove inventory without understanding why it is there. Removing inventory exposes process variation, so if you have problems with suppliers or internal processes, and if you remove inventory too early, you can easily end up with machines or processes stopping due to shortages.

Don't forget other departments can contribute to the lean program. They can also contribute to preventing you from becoming lean. For example:

- Sales or Marketing can look for too much finished goods stock or too many options; you end up with a lot of WIP or very short lead times that result in having to stock excessive inventory).

- Purchasing departments want to meet the no "sock-out" KPI, so they buy excessive stocks of raw materials, or they are afraid of relying on one or two suppliers for key components so they set up multiple suppliers. You can see in this latter example that sometimes KPIs are two sides of the same coin. It is "leaner" to have fewer suppliers, with the risk that a key supplier can close down or be bought by a competitor? Do we get better prices from a supplier if we have higher order volumes or if we let them know there is another supplier involved?

- Finance might like us to have a lot of raw material stock at the start of a month but little at the end.

- Logistics might want to group deliveries or containers together; this helps them meet KPI but can result in stock remaining in the warehouse for longer than necessary.

- IT might have complicated processes, systems that are not user-friendly, or excessively restrictive policies.

- HR might have too many policies, forms that are too long, or procedures that are too cumbersome.

For the above reasons, lean should be considered a KPI for most managers. Everyone should have an interest in removing waste from their department. If it's a KPI, then it should be reviewed to ensure the work done has delivered real and permanent benefits. Sometimes, processes have a tendency to slip back to the old ways, and we can end up with situations where the same project is repeated a few years later because of this slippage.

Quality and lean belong together in that any process that is inefficient or ineffective is not a quality process—it produces waste. A key role of the quality professional is to look at removing this waste.

I am a strong supporter of the theory of constraints (TOC) approach. This looks at throughput (of documents or materials) and bottlenecks. One very small example of this approach is to look for the biggest build-up of inventory on the factory floor. This shows where the bottleneck is; if you want more output, the restrictions of this bottleneck must be removed by adding a second piece of equipment, adding an extra shift, or improving machine efficiency. Eli Goldratt has written several books on this subject, probably the most well-known being *The Goal*. This book, like others in the series, is written in the style of a novel. This makes his books much more interesting to read.

CHAPTER SUMMARY

In this chapter we looked at some of the main components that go into a lean program, we looked at the concept of value-add versus non value-add, and we introduced the theory of constraints.

Questions

1. Do you have a lean program in place? What areas is it addressing?

2. Who is involved in the lean program? Why aren't all departments involved in removing waste from their own processes?

3. Have previous lean programs delivered real benefits? If they have, did you celebrate and reward those involved?

4. Are lean objectives part of every manager's KPIs?

CHAPTER SIXTEEN

✳ ✳ ✳

Six Sigma

CHAPTER OUTLINE:

There are already a multitude of books and courses about Six Sigma, and I don't intend to make this situation worse. In this chapter, we take a more critical view of Six Sigma (6S); rather than focussing on the benefits (or alleged benefits), we look at some of the controversial aspects of introducing a 6S program. We go through some of the concerns and criticisms of 6S, and we highlight the risks of making 6S compulsory, where it can become an end in and of itself. The law of unintended consequences is at play here.

Six Sigma is closely associated with Quality and it is a popular tool in the quality professional's toolkit. Many job postings for quality engineers and managers look for a Six Sigma qualification, but it usually reads as though it has been added in because it's the current trend.

I suspect there are many organizations where the potential benefits of Six Sigma have not materialized, or have materialized only on paper. This could be due to a number of reasons:

- Top management not fully understanding the commitment involved.

- Poor choice of projects.

- Departure of the black belt person, who may be the only one on site.

- Resource constraints. People are expected to dedicate a reasonable percentage of their time to a Six Sigma project while doing everything else they normally do.

- Black belts measured on the number of projects they manage, rather than on the quality and long-term effectiveness of projects.

- A Six Sigma project handed over to the process owner. This can be a problem if the process owner was sidelined by the Six Sigma team. Do process owners and users know what was changed and why? If not, they may just go back to what they used to do.

- If we find a situation where a second or third Six Sigma project is being done on the same problem, we need to stop and investigate why.

There are other concerns with Six Sigma:

- It creates an elite group of people who are the problem definers and solvers. Although there is some participation by employees, it is not nearly enough. I don't want see a 300-person organization with three black belts; I want to see an organization with 300 problem solvers.

- Because of the perceived elite status, ordinary employees can feel left out or be afraid to say things in meetings. It is normal to feel reluctant to speak when you hear people using foreign terms and talking in jargon and about things you know nothing about—special causes, regression analysis, and chi square testing.

- It can lead to a lack of ownership on the part of the people doing the job. This can also apply to the supervisor or manager.

- It can be argued that the real experts are those who are doing the job.

- It can sometimes require continuing external support to maintain the advances made.

- The cost of training is very high. What do we do if our black belt leaves, start again?

- Does it go against the philosophy of smaller, continual improvement projects?

- Six Sigma is applied common sense, with plenty of statistics thrown in. We may already be using many of the Six Sigma tools. Maybe that is sufficient?

- It can result in people delaying normal corrective or preventive actions until their next Six Sigma project is due. People start shelving actions they should be taking because are looking for a Six Sigma project.

- The quality of projects can become poorer over time as low-hanging fruit is gone but people are still expected to complete a certain number of projects. This is especially evident in non-manufacturing situations. Here you can see projects that should never have become a project. Savings projected with many projects decreases over time.

* People often pursue Six Sigma training just to have it on their resumé.

Six Sigma tends to be project-based, with a narrow focus. Its goal is to reduce variation. It models the process, turning a real situation into a statistical model, using data to analyze that model, coming up with a solution, and then transferring that model back into the real world.

You cannot implement Six Sigma in a vacuum, nor should you impose it on an organization and expect good results. What you'll get is people transferring what they would have done by other means into Six Sigma projects. This can result in expensive delays. The culture must be right to get the most from Six Sigma.

Does getting your green or black belt make you a good Six Sigma practitioner? There is more involved than statistics—good project selection, judgement, getting on with people, persuading, knowing which battles to fight.

Why have organizations just accepted that Six Sigma is the way to go? I am all in favor of the tools and techniques used in Six Sigma, but I'm not sure we have to give something a new label, use foreign language terms, and create layers of bureaucracy (white belt, yellow belt, green belt, black belt, master black belt).

We get too focussed on Six Sigma as a panacea for all of our problems rather than focus on what we are trying to achieve with it.

Six Sigma should not be a dictated from the top. There are plenty of valid tools, and some tools are more suitable to various situations; by forcing people to use particular tools and approaches, we may actually be hampering the effectiveness of employee actions.

It's plainly wrong when people are obliged to do a certain number of projects per year. Problems that should be tackled quickly are now delayed while employees focus on preparation and paperwork for the project.

I have seen situations where Six Sigma becomes an end in and of itself, with its own KPIs and even its own department. This epitomizes what is wrong with quality—it's not embedded in people's work and it becomes a separate and specialized process. We don't need KPIs for Six Sigma—every department already has its own KPIs—we just need to improve department performance, irrespective of using Six Sigma or any other approach.

Would it not be better to focus all departments on small improvements, for example a 1% improvement per quarter on their KPIs?

The core focus should be on reducing waste and non-value adding (NVA) activities, reducing the variation of inputs and outputs, mistake proofing, Pareto analysis, and training and involving everyone.

Finally, to balance the argument, I must say that there are many instances where using Six Sigma has resulted in significant benefits for an organization in terms of cost avoidance or cost savings. What I am trying to show in this chapter is that we should not just jump on the Six Sigma bandwagon. A lot of so-called "projects" could and should be tackled straight away without the need for extensive statistics or expensive training. We need to look at what is appropriate for each situation; if we decide to go down the Six Sigma route, we should understand why we have done so.

CHAPTER SUMMARY

In this chapter, we took a critical eye to how Six Sigma is set up in organizations and we considered the law of unintended consequences. The purpose of this chapter is to encourage us to take a fresh look at the hype surrounding 6S, and to question whether we are really getting the benefits we think we are.

Questions

1. Is Six Sigma mandatory in your organization? Why?
2. Do you properly review the results of projects to see whether saving or cost avoidance was achieved?
3. Would any Six Sigma project be just as well handled by other methods, and perhaps completed earlier?
4. Are people delaying projects just to ensure they can meet the KPI requiring one project per year?
5. Is the quality of projects decreasing?
6. Why is it almost assumed that Six Sigma is the only way to improve?

CHAPTER SEVENTEEN

* * *

Risk Management

CHAPTER OUTLINE:

This chapter is an introduction to the concept of risk management and its key components. We outline the risk management process and we look at Failure Modes and Effects Analysis as a risk management tool. We also refer to ISO 31000, which is the ISO standard for risk management.

Risk is unavoidable in our personal and work lives. Every organization faces risks, and it is our job to manage these risks by applying forward thinking and using an agreed framework for dealing with identified risks. Risk management is about trying to avoid or minimize uncertainty. Risks have aspects and effects:

- Aspect: financial, environmental, health and safety, etc.

- Effects: positive or negative, in all cases deviation from the norm.

Risk management process

There are many flow charts available online showing the risk management process, including in the standard ISO 31000; most risk management frameworks follow these steps:

- Identification of internal and external context.

- Risk identification—What can happen, where can it happen, and how can it happen (known or foreseeable hazards)? Also consider legal, regulatory, or industry requirements; audit reviews, changes to equipment, personnel, etc. Risks can arise from the internal environment (material shortages, downtime, absenteeism, training) and external environment (currency fluctuations, new competitors), so both need to be considered.

- Risk analysis—Determine the likelihood and consequences of something going wrong (estimate the risk; assign a value from 1-10 for the seriousness of the hazard and for the likelihood of it occurring). Some organizations just use low-medium-high scoring for likelihood and consequences, because often we cannot be more accurate than that. Giving something a number score does not necessarily mean our analysis is any better than giving something a high score. Ultimately, all we want is a guide to focus our attention on those items that score the highest; we should not get into an argument over whether something should have a score of 6 or 7.

- Risk evaluation—Determine the criteria (a threshold risk value) and priorities. We should also be looking at causes and consequences in evaluating risk. How big an impact will the risk have if it happens (financial, environmental, quality, reputational, geographic)?

- Risk detection—How likely and how early are we to detect a problem if something goes wrong?

- Risk action plan—This can consist of one or more of the following:

  - Risk avoidance—Can we avoid or remove the risk in some way?

  - Risk reduction—Identify and implement risk reduction measures (repeat steps (a)-(c) if necessary); risk reduction can reduce probability or impact.

  - Risk acceptance—Is the residual risk acceptable; can we agree on what is acceptable?

  - Risk transference—Can we transfer the risk to another organization or association, one that is better able to handle it (e.g., a specialist chemical treatment organization, a consultant, a supplier, or an industry association)?

- Have any other hazards been created by the introduction of the risk reduction measures?

- Once risks have been identified and scored, the next step is to create an action plan that defines what we are to do and why. This is followed by more detailed steps that define how we are going do it, by when, and by whom.

- Risk review—How effective were our actions? What new threats have appeared since the last review? Go back to (a).

This framework can apply to most types of risk—financial, manufacturing, outsourcing to another organization or country, changing key suppliers, or moving to a sole supplier for a key component or service.

One of the key steps is determining how to weight risks, and there are plenty of weighting scales available online. In most cases, an organization should not try to find or devise an exact weighting table or formula to suit their specific organization. It is better to have a scale that is less precise but is used consistently.

From a strategic standpoint, some of the more common tools include SWOT analysis, PESTLE analysis, the SEEQS approach mentioned in Chapter 5; decision tree analysis, bowtie analysis, or Porter's 5 forces analysis referenced in Chapter 2; and the table shown in Chapter 2 (Table 1—Strategy and quality).

When reviewing risk, we also need to consider:

- The risk of doing nothing.

- Opportunities or "positive" risks.

- The concept of hazard. If a hazard exists but there is little or no likelihood of exposure to that hazard, then the risk is low. For example, as part of a discussions on risk we might say that flooding of our premises is a hazard. But if our facility is not in a flood area or if it is on a hill, the likelihood of being flooded will be low; we can move on to the next item. The hazard still exists but we will not be exposed to it.

A typical risk management table can look something like Table 6.

From a quality perspective, the most common tool used for risk management is Failure Modes and Effects Analysis (FMEA), and it is normally performed for design, product, and process. FMEA looks at specific risks based on severity, occurrence, and detection. Numbers are assigned to these three categories (usually between 1 and 10), these numbers are multiplied together, and the result (called a risk priority number, or RPN) is evaluated against a pre-agreed action limit. This limit will usually be expressed in this form: "if the RPN is greater than x, then preventive and/or corrective action must be taken." These actions are then implemented and the calculation is repeated to look for the highest residual risks.

Table 6 Typical risk management table.

Hazard or process step	A = Probability of hazard happening	B = Severity of hazard	Risk Factor (RF) = A*B	Risk action plan	Action plan status	Action plan due date	Action plan responsible	New probability	New severity	New risk factor

Risk management has become closely aligned with Quality, in the sense that there is usually a risk associated with the quality of our product or service. It is not efficient or profitable to inspect every part produced or every transaction, so there will be a statistical chance of something non-conforming reaching a customer. Prevention is the better way to go, using the various tools discussed throughout this book.

There is an ISO guide on risk management that is useful for most organizations. This standard is "ISO 31000, Risk Management—Principles and Guidelines." There is an associated guide also available, "ISO/IEC 31010, Risk management—Risk assessment techniques."

These are worthwhile publications for senior managers to read and discuss before implementing a risk management strategy. After all, for senior management, risk is a big factor in decision making. At a senior level, the risks considered tend to be more external than internal.

It is important to note that ISO 9001 includes specific references to risk and risk management, so it can be worth considering things like SWOT analyses to the processes in your organization—at all levels. If we adopt a risk management approach, we should review this periodically. And if we want to promote the idea of using risk management tools, maybe we should reward those who do, at least in the early stages.

Risk management is not solely for the quality professional. It can be applied to an organization at every level, including at director level.

CHAPTER SUMMARY

This chapter looked at the concept of risk management and its key components. From a quality point of view, the FMEA is the most commonly used risk management tool. There is also an ISO standard for risk management—ISO 31000. Finally, it should be noted that risk management is now an explicit component of ISO 9001.

Questions

1. Is there a formal risk management approach in your organization?
2. Is risk assessment applied at each level in the organization?
3. Are the results of risk assessment reviewed adequately and is agreed upon action implemented?
4. Do you reward those who drive the risk management process?

APPENDIX 1

***

Definitions of Quality

- ISO 9000 definition: Quality is the characteristic of a product to meet the specified requirements
- Customer satisfaction
- Fit for purpose
- Meeting specifications
- Right first time
- Zero defects
- Reducing variation around a target
- When the customer comes back, not the product
- Meeting customer and regulatory standards
- The characteristics of a product or service that bear on its ability to satisfy stated or implied needs
- What the customer perceives it to be
- The degree to which an item or process meets or exceeds customer requirements and expectations
- How closely a product or service meets its design specification
- A product or service free of deficiencies
- Never having to say you're sorry
- No surprises
- Quality = performance/expectation; must be greater than 1
- The right product, available at the right time, at the right cost, and meeting customer perceived standard/requirements/needs
- Conformance to requirements; can be subjective because requirements vary from person to person

- Doing your job right—first time, on time, all the time
- "Quality goes well beyond satisfying requirements and specifications. It is about anticipating and satisfying expectations. It is about knowing and understanding people. And above all it is about simplicity combined with innovation and ingenuity, a new way of looking at the same and coming up with unexpected simple and creative solutions. In short, it is about always being ahead of the others and setting the requirements others will then strive to satisfy."

As an aside, here is a standard differentiation between Quality Control and Quality Assurance:

- Quality Control (QC) tends to be focussed on products, problem detection, test, inspection.
- Quality Assurance (QA) is more focussed on processes, problem prevention, training, tools, systems, methods.

APPENDIX 2

* * *

A Generic History
of Quality

What follows is my own interpretation of how Quality has developed over the years.

Originally, most items that could be purchased were handmade (or grown), and we relied on the skill and expertise of the craftsman, builder, cook, or blacksmith.

With mechanization and the industrial revolution, jobs became less skilled. In order to maximize productivity, people performed just one part of a job rather than making a complete item or providing a complete service.

Because of the reduction in skill (or rather a reduction in training, and restrictions on what people were allowed to do), people became less likely to "own" what they made and felt less responsible for the finished product. This did not help the quality of a product. Following on from this, it became necessary to check what people had made.

This resulted in having people whose job it was to check the quality of the products made. These were called quality controllers and they inspected the products. A lot of time and money was spent on inspection because no-one felt confident that there was control over the process. A product might be good today but bad tomorrow.

The inspection process became quite sophisticated and used various techniques such as sampling tables and acceptance levels. This way of working was fine for many years but it had several flaws. For example:

- It further alienated the people who made the product. They felt less and less responsible for it. After all, it was Quality Control's job to check it and find the faults. This eventually resulted in the situation where people felt QC was responsible for quality.

- The tendency was to focus on the final product rather than the stages in between. By the time something was found to be wrong, it was often too late to correct it. Although the fault may not have reached the customer, the level of rejects became an expensive item.

- The focus was on the product or service and not on the processes that were involved in making the product. At best, even with 100 % inspection, faulty parts were produced before any action was taken.

- Customers found it was necessary to have a quality inspection team to check anything that was purchased. This was expensive and non-value-adding. To complicate matters further, each customer usually had a different inspection and acceptance criteria.

- Even with 100% inspection, non-conforming product still reached customers.

Wouldn't it be nice if we could do something to change this situation?

- Find problems before they occur.

- Measure and correct processes to minimize the chances of nonconforming product being made or a poor service being provided.

- Have a common system for ensuring that certain core competence criteria were met.

- Detect non-conformances earlier in the process, ideally at the station they were made.

Thus was born the era of:

- Process monitoring and measurement.

- The desire to have a common generic standard to demonstrate compliance. This resulted in the ISO 9001 standard. The benefit of having this standard was that organizations could rely on an independent company auditing the quality systems of suppliers, thus eliminating the necessity to visit and audit them individually. It also meant that suppliers didn't have to have all their customers coming in to audit them. It was win-win.

But there were some drawbacks:

- The auditing company was being paid by the company being audited. This resulted in an inherent conflict of interest.

- The quality of independent auditors and certification companies varies, so customer organizations were not always getting a consistent result.

- ISO 9001 was by its very nature generic, but this meant that it didn't delve deeply enough for certain industries (aviation, automotive, medical device, telecommunications). The end result was that those industries had to develop their own extensions to ISO 9001. They still relied on certification bodies to do the auditing, so they did not have to go back to the old system of auditing individual suppliers.

Today, many companies are happy to deal with suppliers who have ISO 9001 certification, yet there many do not rely on it as a means of ensuring quality. One of the reasons for this is that ISO 9001 is a systems framework; its focus was never on product quality. In order to focus on product quality, it would be necessary to address requirements of every product, thus making the standard unusable. Let's not blame ISO for the approach taken. It was the best that could be done.

APPENDIX 3

* * *

Traditional Key Performance Indicators for Quality

- Number of out-of-spec issues raised / resolved, per month
- Number of repeat audit non-conformances raised / closed, internal and external (customer and any certification or regulatory bodies)
- Process compliance
- Number of process innovations
- Reduction in scrap rates (%)
- Cost of poor quality (CoPQ)—internal appraisal, prevention, internal failure costs
- Continual improvements—amount saved or not expended
- Internal right first time
- Response time / closure time for customer complaints
- Time to close audit non-conformances
- Number of supplier corrective action requests (CARs)
- Number of repeat faults—supplier issues, internal complaints
- Number of items out of calibration
- Number of improvement projects and process innovations, and their value
- Number of (major) non-conformances to the standard used
- Monthly comparison of audit results
- Third-party (customer or certification body) audit results
- Number of product recalls
- Amount of rework
- Amount of retest

- Amount of re-inspection
- Supplier assessment results
- Value of old or damaged stock scrapped
- Successful initial sample inspection reports
- Amount of scrap—by number or value
- Process capability studies conducted
- Customer satisfaction/feedback ratings (target top 3)
- Response times, close-out times to customer issues
- Number of customers lost
- Error % for any process step
- Reduction in scrap, increase in yield
- Overall equipment effectiveness (OEE)
- Training, level of cross training, number of trainers on site
- Prevention costs

APPENDIX 4

Flow Chart
Procedure Template

Note: Photos, diagrams, and drawings can be added to relevant sections of the flow chart (see Figure 15 on next page).

	Doc. No.:		Issue Date:	
	Issue:		Page:	of
		Printed version only valid only on:		20-Mar-2017

TITLE:

PURPOSE:

SCOPE:

RESPONSIBILITY:

RELATED DOCUMENTS:
RELATED PROCEDURES:
RELATED FORMS:

Relevant ISO 9001 clauses:

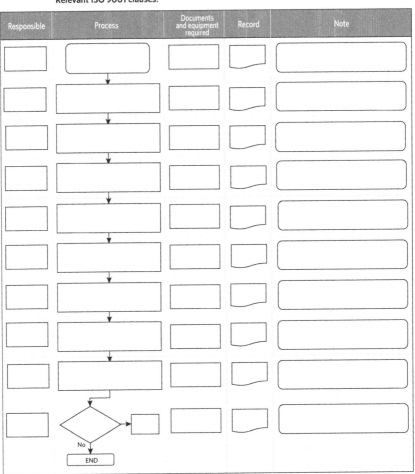

Figure 15 Flowchart procedure template.

APPENDIX 5

* * *

Risk Tool— Failure Mode and Effects Analysis (FMEA)

There are many books and resources available on FMEA. This is a brief overview of how the tool is used (see Table 7 on next page).

Starting at "process step," we calculate the RPN (risk priority number) by multiplying the figures we insert against severity, occurrence, and detection. This is done for the "current RPN." Usually we set a threshold value (it might be 50 or 100), and we decide that anything over this threshold value needs action. If the calculation is less than the threshold value, we take no further action. Where action is required and has been taken, we enter new values for occurrence and detection. The value for severity often remains unchanged (The effect on the customer is the same whether the problem gets to them before or after action is taken; from a customer's point of view, he has the same issue.) Then we recalculate the RPN (the "new RPN") to see whether any values exceed the threshold. If necessary, we repeat the process.

Table 7 FMEA (failure mode and effects analysis).

Process Step	Function	Failure Mode	Failure Effect	Potential Failure Cause or Failure Mechanism	Current Process Controls	Class	Engineering Change Number, Complaint Number, Audit Number	Severity (S)	Occurrence (O)	Detection (D)	Preventive action	Detection action	Current RPN = S x O x D	Recommended actions	Do the actions eliminate or avoid, reduce, or mitigate the risk?	Responsibility	Due date	Actions taken	Severity (S)—same value as above	Occurrence (O)	Detection (D)	New RPN = old S x new O x new D

APPENDIX 6

* * *

Abbreviations

Abbreviation	Explanation
5S	Sort, Straighten, Shine, Standardize, Sustain
6S	Six Sigma
8D	8 Disciplines
AMP	Autonomy, Mastery, and Purpose
ANOVA	Analysis of Variance
APQP	Advanced Product Quality Planning
AQL	Acceptable Quality Level
BB	Black belt
BMS	Business Management System
BPR	Business Process Re-engineering
BSC	Balanced ScoreCard
CAPA	Corrective and Preventive Action
CAR	Corrective Action Request
CB	Certification Body
CoC	Certificate of Conformance
CoPQ	Cost of Poor Quality
CoQ	Cost of Quality
CSR	Corporate Social Responsibility
CTQ	Critical to Quality
DFA	Design for Assembly
DFM	Design for Manufacture

Abbreviation	Explanation
DFMEA	Design Failure Modes and Effects Analysis
DFS	Design for Service
DFU	Design for Use
DOE	Design of Experiments
DPMO	Defects Per Million Opportunities
ERP	Enterprise Resource Planning
FFA	Force Field Analysis
FG	Finished Goods
FIFO	First in, First out
FMEA	Failure Modes and Effects Analysis
FRS	Functional Requirement Specification
GB	Green Belt
HR	Human Resources
IRR	Internal Rate of Return
ISIR	Initial Sample Inspection Report
IT	Information Technology
JIT	Just in Time
KPI	Key Performance Indicator
MBWA	Management by Walking Around
MSA	Measurement System Analysis
NC	Non-conformance
NOK	Not OK
NPI	New Product Introduction
NPV	Net Present Value
NVA	Non-Value Added
OEE	Overall Equipment Effectiveness
OMS	Organization Management System
OOS	Out of Specification
OTD	On Time Delivery
QFD	Quality Function Deployment

Abbreviation	Explanation
QRQC	Quick Response Quality Control
PAR	Preventive Action Request
PDCA	Plan Do Check Act
PESTLE	Political, Economic, Social, Technological, Environmental, Legal
PFMEA	Process Failure Modes and Effects Analysis
P/N	Part Number
PPAP	Production Part Approval Process
PPM	Parts Per Million
QA	Quality Assurance
QC	Quality Control
QMS	Quality Management System
RCA	Root Cause Analysis
ROA	Return on Assets
ROI	Return on Investment
RPN	Risk Priority Number
SC	Special Characteristics
SCAR	Supplier Corrective Action Request
SEEQS	Safe, Ethical, Environmentally friendly, ensures Quality, Sustainable
SIPOC	Supplier, Input, Process, Output, Customer
SLA	Service Level Agreement
SMED	Single Minute Exchange of Dies
SOP	Standard Operating Procedure
SPC	Statistical Process Control
STEP	Social, Technological, Economic and Political
SWOT	Strengths, Weaknesses, Opportunities, Threats
TIMWOOD	Transport, Inventory, Movement, Waste, Overproduction, Overprocessing, Defects
TPM	Total Predictive Maintenance
TOC	Theory of Constraints

Abbreviation	Explanation
TQM	Total Quality Management
URS	User Requirement Specification
VOC	Voice of the Customer
VSM	Value Stream Mapping
WI	Work Instruction
WIP	Work in Progress
ZD	Zero Defects

APPENDIX 7

* * *

Quality Tools

This book does not review the multitude of quality tools in existence. This has been done by many authors previously and there are ample resources available online.

New tools are "invented" often. Why? We seem to be always looking for the next big thing, the next item that will solve our problems. Although it is obvious that certain tools are essential and have stood the test of time, we should be critically asking whether the "newer" tools generate the extra benefit we desire. There seems to be a "one-upmanship" philosophy at play, where we are eager to be seen at the forefront using new techniques. I suggest that we should first ask this question. Will this new tool give me anything different to what I am currently using?

Below, I have listed some of the main tools that are used and categorized them to make the application of them easier. I have found that this helps clarify when to apply the many tools and techniques in existence.

As with many things, the 80/20 rule applies. Certain tools are indispensable to most organizations. These include:

- 5 whys or a decision tree
- Fishbone diagram
- Pareto analysis
- Trend graphs
- 8D*
- FMEA and Control Plan

8D is discussed in more detail later in this appendix.

Tools

- **For root cause analysis:** 5 whys, fishbone diagram, brainstorming, Pareto chart, scatter diagram, is/is not table, fault tree analysis, Six Sigma, flow chart, 5Whys/2Hows + what has changed. 5 whys is not the best tool to use whe the cause is not known, and there is a tendency to assume that each symptom has only one root cause. A way of approaching this is:
  - Define the problem (what is it and what are the symptoms?)
  - Collect and analyze data (get the evidence—how long has the problem existed, where does it occur; identify and investigate possible causal factors—what sequence of events led to the problem, what conditions allow the problem to occur; use 5 whys)
  - Identify the root causes and potential solution (get proof of this)
  - Recommend and implement solutions (*who, what, where, when,* and *how* feed into the FMEA, and the Control Plan and SOP)
  - Standardize and monitor
- **For data collection and analysis:** Pareto, histograms, SPC, check sheet, sampling, Design Of Experiments, control chart, scatter diagram, survey, stratification, trend chart, flow chart, process mapping, 5 whys, tree diagram, ANOVA (analysis of variance)
- **For continual improvement:** Pareto, Six Sigma, FMEA, lean, CAPA, control charts, the concept of the internal customer, Zero Defects, Total Predictive Maintenance (TPM), Theory of Constraints (TOC), SIPOC, 5 whys, Value Stream Management, mistake proofing, Total Quality Management, cross functional teams, quality circles, SPC.
- **For corrective action:** 8D (see page 178)—add in tools or approaches that might be appropriate at each stage: Six Sigma, A3 reporting, Quick Response Quality Control (QRQC), mistake proofing, visual controls, quality circles. Use the control loop concept—feedback and feed forward. The employee needs to know asap if something is wrong, inspection analysis—mark up the faults on a drawing—which will show the most frequent areas affected.
- **For preventive action:** FMEA, SPC, capability studies, customer feedback, supplier feedback, mistake proofing, Total Quality Management.

- **For mistake proofing:** eliminate the error-causing step, or replace the step. Minimize by—inspection method (successive inspection, self-inspection by employee, source inspection, auto inspection), setting (sensor, count, weigh), regulatory function (buzzer, light, jigs).

- **For reducing time and movement, improving efficiency, and spotting missing items quickly:** 5S—Sort (need, don't need), Set in order (a place for everything), Shine (clean first), Standardize (ground rules), Sustain (audit).

- **For reality charting:** Causal reality has at least two causes—an action (causal factors) and a condition or conditions (contribute to the occurrence of the problem but are not the initiating cause). The conditions need drilling down to find root causes.

- **For visual systems:** Colored labels/packaging/pallets/material; various material sizes; similar parts stored in particular locations (incoming as well as WIP and FG); various weights, color coding, specific locations for particular material types; maybe P/Ns are too similar and get mixed.

Plan-Do-Check-Act

Plan-Do-Check-Act has been a cornerstone for the concept of introducing and monitoring quality changes. There are several variations of this.

P—Determine goals and targets, and methods of reaching these.

D—Engage in training and education, implement the work.

C—Check the effects of implementation.

A—Take appropriate action.

Statistical Process Control (SPC)

Interfering with systems that only exhibit common cause variation can create special causes by the actions we take. We don't try to correct variation in a process that is in statistical control unless we know it is common cause and we want to improve the overall system. If the process is in statistical control, then the problem is a fault of the system. If the process is not in statistical control, it means there are special causes present; these need to be eliminated by means of SPC charting and capability studies before moving on to look at the common causes.

8D process:

The 8D process is usually broken down as follows:

- Problem identification. Is it new or a repeated problem? If it's a repeat problem, we can refer to previous data as well as new data.

- Problem description. Get the details—photos, part number and revision, quantity, when the issue was first observed, serial numbers, batch numbers or work order numbers, time to failure. Answer the *what, where, when,* and *how* of the issue.

- Containment/short term corrective action. How much stock could be affected—in our warehouse, going through our process, in a staging warehouse, or in transit to the customer? Do we need to introduce 100% inspection to ensure the problem does not reach the customer until we implement our full corrective action? How many parts does the customer have? If we think it is a problem from our suppliers, we need to ask the same questions from them.

- Possible root causes. Use tools such as 5 whys, brainstorming, fishbone diagram, Pareto chart, scatter diagram, is/is not, fault tree analysis, Six Sigma, flow chart, 5Whys/2Hows + what has changed. Make sure to delve deeper than the "symptom level."

- Root cause(s) and corrective action(s). Identify root causes and determine appropriate corrective action.

- Corrective action. Verify that action has been effective in eliminating the problem, that it addresses the root cause identified. Will the actions prevent recurrence? Have we considered other products or processes that could suffer from similar issues, and have we applied corrective actions to them? Have the actions inadvertently created other issues? Have we updated our documentation (FMEA, control plans, work instructions, user guides)?

- Future-proofing action. Have we embedded the actions above? How do we ensure these actions are still in place when we introduce new or modified products or processes that could suffer from the same problem? Has the issue been communicated to the Design department? Review inspection data to confirm the issue has not recurred. If we have more than one facility, have we shared our results with the other facilities?

- Congratulate the team and publish the success.

A Note on Project Management

A project management approach can be helpful when making changes to a process or quality system. Much of what quality professionals do can be thought of as small projects—a Six Sigma project, redefining how inspection is carried out, carrying out FMEAs, and so on. There are several standard tools used in project management, including:

- Risk assessment
- Cost benefit analysis
- Critical path analysis
- Gantt charts
- Ranking, prioritising, via:
  - Net present value (NPV)
  - Internal rate of return (IRR)
  - Return on investment (ROI)
  - Return on assets (ROA)
  - Payback period
  - Break-even analysis

Because most projects involve teams, it is beneficial to understand group dynamics. Most teams have a common purpose and approach and are accountable for results.

Successful project management includes things such as:

- Developing trust within the group.
- Deciding how issues will be resolved within the group. Do we need unanimity?
- Having a clear vision. Why does this group exist?
- Having a clear mission. Where do we want to get to?
- Having a clear strategy. How will we get there?
- Having clear values. What are the principles and beliefs that lead to behavior?
- Understanding the constraints. Financial, people, time, information, equipment.
- Determining the targets and milestones.

- Assigning responsibility for each action.
- Determining project boundaries.
- Recognizing individual levels of commitment.
- Assuring good team balance.
- Assessing team members' buy-in for project.
- Determining project priorities. Time, quality, cost.
- Anticipating projected benefits.
- Where are the determining project gates and handovers at key stages.

An early success can help a team gel and generate more support throughout the organization. To make team members feel special give small rewards, empower them, trust them, give them authority and resources. The ideal situation exists when there are more people wanting to be on the team than there are spaces available.

Eli Goldratt has written a good book on the topic of project management, *Critical Chain*, which follows the Theory of Constraints philosophy.

* * *

Bibliography

Babbitt, Tripp. Tripp Babbitt's Blog.

Brewster, David. *Success with Simplicity.* Monterey Press (2005).

Crosby, Philip. *Quality is Free.* Signet Books (1987).

Deming, W. Edwards. *Out of the Crisis.* MIT (1986).

Goldratt, Eli. *Critical Chain.* Routledge (1997).

Goldratt, Eli. *The Goal.* Routledge (2004).

Maromonte, Kevin R. *Building the Invisible Quality Corporation.* Quorum Books (1996).

Mickelwright, Mike. *Lean ISO 9001.* ASQ Quality Press (2010).

Moon, Jon. *Clarity and Impact.* Oberon Publishing (2016).

Moon, Jon. *How to Make an Impact.* Financial Times/Prentice Hall (2007).

Pink, Daniel H. *Drive: The Surprising Truth About What Motivates Us.* Canongate Books (2011).

The Vanguard Method (www.vanguard-method.com).

***

About the Author

Fin Rooney graduated with a Mechanical Engineering degree from the Dublin Institute of Technology and later completed an MBA with the Open University.

He has worked in several manufacturing and service organizations including Cummins Power Generation, FCI Connect, Sanmina Corporation, RPS Engineering Services, No Climb Products Ltd., and Wexford Electronix, holding roles of Quality Engineer, Quality Manager, Commercial Manager, and Quality Leader. He has also run his own organization, providing quality consultancy, quality outsourcing, quality auditing, and quality training.

He has been a member of the National Standards Authority of Ireland (NSAI) QMS committee, the Irish committee that looks at ISO 9001 developments and standards.

Fin has worked with leading organizations in Ireland and the UK and is a member of the American Society for Quality (ASQ), The Chartered Quality Institute (CQI), The Chartered Management Institute (CMI), and Engineers Ireland (EI).

Fin has assisted organizations in achieving ISO 9001 certification and has set up a Quality department in a new facility. He has achieved customer certification from companies such as Renault, JCB, Hyster-Yale Group, and Mitsubishi Caterpillar Forklift Europe. He has also helped organizations reduce defect levels and streamline documentation, and has introduced visual controls in various organizations.

He has had two articles published previously, one on an introduction to statistical process control (SPC) and a second on ISO 9001 for small organizations.

Fin is from Ireland but currently lives and works in the UK. His website is www.finrooney.com. He can also be contacted via LinkedIn at www.linkedin.com/in/finrooney.

* * *

Index

Note: page numbers in *italics* indicate figures and tables.